THE COOL
APPLE EXPRESS

THE COOL APPLE EXPRESS

Michael J. Hicks

STONEWALL PRESS
PAVING YOUR WAY TO SUCCESS

The Cool Apple Express
Copyright © 2018 by Michael J. Hicks. All rights reserved.
First published by AuthorHouse 11/29/2011

No part of this publication may be reproduced, stored in a retrieval system or transmitted in any way by any means, electronic, mechanical, photocopy, recording or otherwise without the prior permission of the author except as provided by USA copyright law.

The opinions expressed by the author are not necessarily those of Stonewall Press.

Published in the United States of America

ISBN: 978-1-64460-017-7 (*sc*)
      978-1-64460-016-0 (*e*)

Library of Congress Control Number: 2018959611

Published by Stonewall Press
4800 Hampden Lane, Suite 200, Bethesda, MD 20814 USA
1.888.334.0980 | www.stonewallpress.com

Memoirs (Biography/Autobiography)
18.11.29

CONTENTS

Introduction 7
This Is Where It Began 13
Working My Way Into Trucking 25
Up In Port Angeles 51
1972   All Over The Place Like A Fart In A Skillet 55
1973   Lots Of Driving And A Few Odd Encounters 63
1974   Another Mixed Bag 71
1975   Wonder Bread 81
C F Tanklines 87
A Good Place To Work But Bad Equipment—Good People 87
Pulled The Pin At C F Tanklines 95
Making A Decision And 4 Years At Lone Star 105
Post Lone Star The Next 3 Years And Sanity 117
Two And A Half Years Of Starting Over 137
Working At Boeing Trucking 147
Epilogue 161

INTRODUCTION

"Don't compare your life to others, You have no idea what their journey is all about."

"A woman marries a man expecting he will change, but he doesn't. A man marries a woman expecting that she won't change, but she does."

THE COOL APPLE EXPRESS is not a real trucking company that I ever knew of but, it has been in my mind pushing 40 years at this point. Starting on 4th of July weekend 1971, I made my first sleeper trip of all time, running from Seattle to Chicago. Over the next 6 years, I would haul a lot of apples from areas in Eastern Washington to the Twin-Cities, and the greater Chicago area. It wasn't the only product I would haul but, it was a product I would haul a lot of, that was very popular. During that period of time, I came real close, about 3 times, to buying my own rig and running that route. I had the name; the design, and the colors for all of the equipment I would own, imbedded in my brain all these years. So, when I made the decision to write my book, I already knew what the name of it would be, and what the graphics would look like. In the short term, it may have been a good idea, but over the long term, and being able to look back in time, it was to my unconscious luck that I opted out. I know with just one rig, and not getting the itch to get bigger, or, bad luck, I most likely would have done real well. I was very disciplined with my work ethic and proper operation and care of the equipment I drove, but the constant grind over the years, and the responsibility to keep the wheels going 7 days a week, probably would have taken its toll over time, and I would have either sold out or bailed.

There is a certain rush and feeling of independence when you are doing this particular kind of work, maybe a little different in real life, than what is portrayed in movies or stories. Even if you don't own the rig you are driving, once you pull out the gate and the wheels are on the highway, you're pretty much the boss, there is no one looking over your shoulder. You are expected to think on your feet, and make quick decisions with no one to hold your hand. Lots of weather related conditions dictate what you have to do, and there is always going to be equipment problems to deal with. Over the years I have had a few friends that were killed on the road, all experienced drivers. I've had some close calls myself but, considering all the things that could have happened, I feel fortunate and I thank the Good Lord for that. Going into the ditch up on Bozeman Hill one time in extremely slick conditions will be a memory I'll have the rest of my life. Coming off Stevens Pass west bound with a pneumatic tanker and losing my air, same story, I shudder just thinking about it. One time at night, crossing the desert between LA and Phoenix, I dozed at the wheel momentarily, when I opened my eyes and regained my senses, I got a Volvo pedaling as fast as he can right in front of me going down Banning Hill. One more second and it could have been disaster. That one instance always reminds me of that old 1940 movie, a trucking classic called "They Drive by night".

You drive long enough, you will experience many things like this, unless of course, you live a charmed life.

Everything I have edited in this book is absolutely true, and I have worded in my own unprofessional style. I would not be comfortable with a ghost writer, it would not seem like the real thing. I am not un-educated, but I am anything but a real author and my story needs to be told in my own words.

The Cool Apple Express

I could have never have been as successful as I was to become the accomplished driver I am, if it were not for a few special people. Also, I want to thank some people for giving me certain opportunities along the way, opportunities that were valuable in reaching a plane of existence making life a lot easier.

First of all, I probably should mention my lifelong pal Roger "Rocky" Hannan, one of the first people I tied up with when I came back from Texas in June 1965. I would ride with him at work, and felt the desire to learn the trade. He was driving a brand new 1965 Autocar with a 5X4, 2O gears, and I had almost zero knowledge in the very beginning. So, just like Rock always said from that day on, "You're startin' directly from the top". I didn't learn overnight. Rock had been driving since he was 18, and he came from a family of truck drivers. He took a tanker over Snoqualmie Pass alone at the age of 18. He, his whole family, and all his close friends, were driver fanatics, and that is a good thing for the long haul. I was called a lot of names, and made to feel real bad a lot of times, till it was beaten into my head, and that was the real payoff, and like I said, it didn't happen overnight.

Another special person that was instrumental in finessing my driving ability was Rocky's, and my friend, Craig Stewart. I met Craig at the very same time I started riding with Rock, he and Craig were driving for the same guy. It would be 6 years up the road in 1971, when I made my first sleeper trip, and it was with Craig. Craig was an excellent driver, a perfectionist, and the trip I made to Chicago and back with him was a tremendous education for me too. Thank you Craig, thank you very much. I used those skills you taught me the rest of my driving career.

I learned driving skills from other people along the way, some are no longer alive. I had a driving partner for a while named Ben Fabens. Ben was a very accomplished driver that had just about seen it all. I learned driving skills while driving with Ben, that, I probably would not pick up from the average person. He was real good at driving in adverse winter conditions, and that would pay off for me so many times I can't remember. One of the questions I asked him that would really payoff for me was, what to do if a front tire blows at freeway speed, fully loaded. Sure enough, the day would come when I needed that answer. I was running east bound on I-84, south side of the Columbia River past Biggs Junction. I was doing at least 60mph, a brand new Firestone front blew, I had the drill imbedded in my brain. I kept it straight, got it off the road. A "Willis Shaw" truck spotted me sitting on the side of the road with the tractor leaning to the left. They stopped, crossed over and drove me back to Biggs Junction. Good guys! I had the garage bring their entire tire truck down. Took the two best trailer tires I had, take the other Firestone front off too, strapped both tires on the flatbed, put the two trailer tires on the front of my tractor. I was coming back from California, went on in to Spokane to unload and load, and on back to Seattle. I couldn't wait to tell the boss about them new Firestone fronts!

Some of the people along the way that need mention, and people I want to thank for hiring me, maybe at important times, I will list them here. Joe Penberthy (now deceased), that hired me against his own better judgement, he thought, but did anyway. Jim Salvatore (now deceased), he hired me at System Transfer and became a friend of mine; I really liked Jim. Dale Leik at SeaBay Transportation. Dale and I were never very close, but Dale was always nice to me, I bird dogged him over a period of time before he hired me. Dale was OK. Thank you Dale. Ken Bouden—Boeing supervisor. In the 6½ years I was at Boeing trucking before I retired, there wasn't anybody thought more highly of in conversation than Ken. He hired me but …not without the prompting of two Union business agents, my good friend Tim Sullivan, and also Ed Seils, they put in a good word for me, and it paid off. I really appreciated that, especially at that particular time. Bob Dinsmore, dispatcher at LASME all the time I was there, turned me on to the job at Olympic Foundry. That was a long, long time ago, but I never forgot the best Dispatcher I ever worked for. You were the best Bobby!

I can't name everybody I've known in my lifetime, and I don't want to leave anyone out that deserves mention. Thank you, thank you all you good and dear people.

Mike & Rocky in front of Turner's Grocery
13th & S. W. Holden Street. Fall of 1944

Mike & Rocky in front of Mike's Mother's house in 1977

THIS IS WHERE IT BEGAN

We have to start somewhere and the first of June 1956 is a good place to start. I graduated from Hi School on that date at the age of 18. My Mother drove down from Seattle with a good friend of mine, Ralph Prosceno, to see me walk across the stage and get my diploma. There was a lot of green, and so much had transpired from the day I started my freshman year till I made it to the finish line at St Martins High School in Olympia, Washington. In that period of time, I would lose my Dad; my Grandpa, and actually lose my Mother for a while. I would come to realize when I got a little older, the 2 years I spent at St. Martins would be the one best thing that would happen to me in my lifetime.

Before I go any farther, it's important that I add some humor in the beginning of this true story, my journal. It starts out with quite a few hard knocks, and for the average stranger that might start reading this, it's possible they could get turned off early. I feel there are a lot of humorous events as you get along into the journal, but I am going to pre-empt early with a funny story.

We have to fast forward to 1977 and the big piano move. My life long best friend Rocky & I were involved in a later day edition of Stan & Ollies piano move from back in the 30's. I'm sure even the youngest generation knows of "Laurel & Hardy." The one where the whole film is about the foils of getting the piano up the huge flight of stairs only to find out at the end of the movie they could have driven up the hill around to the back door. The name of the movie is, "The Music Box". There was this 1916 Stark upright player piano in my family going as far back as… 1916 I guess. It was about as heavy as 3 engine blocks and 50 times bulkier. It had been at one of my Mothers neighbors rec rooms for some years and she wanted it moved to a small studio in West Seattle across the street from "Joe Banana's." My buddy Rock had a real clean 51 Chevy pick-up, and we were going to rent a U-Haul tip trailer and haul it behind his pick-up. I had 3 guys from work that were supposed to show up and help us muscle it on and off. Well… the three guys didn't show, and I found out later they had gone golfing or, something more fun than moving a piano. When they didn't show, Rock said, "hell with them guys, let's just do it ourselves." We got down to the house where the piano was located. You take one look at that piano and wonder how in the hell it got in there to begin with. The owner of the house was a pretty good sized guy, so that helped the two of us. Once we had ripped our sacks getting it onto the trailer and anchored, then we're in business. Neither Rock, or me, had ever seen this studio, but we knew the location.

We left the SandPoint area and headed for California Ave, in West Seattle. The bed of the truck was empty, and the piano was tall and heavy in that little trailer. We were getting a lot of action going around curves, up and down hills. It was comical to us as we were pulling this load across town. We start up Admiral way, and as we bend the corner where the telescopes overlook Elliot Bay, and the city, I look back at the trailer and it's bearing the weight on the passenger side wheel, the driver side wheel is off the ground. Kind of sends a rush through your body for an instant wondering whether it will actually go over, or… come back down. It came back down. We go left on California, at the light, and wave at West Seattle High School as we roll by. I had gone to West Seattle High as a sophomore and, Rocky's older sister & brother had both went to West Seattle High back in the 40's. When we arrived at the

The Cool Apple Express

studio, it looked good at first, we had plenty of room to get it off onto the street and up onto the side walk. It was blind luck that, when we got to the door we had a whole 1 ½ inch clearance on the sides to get thru the door. That's when the real fun started. Just inside the entry door was a mini vestibule followed by another door with a high threshold before you could get into the studio. I'm 6 foot 190 pounds in good shape. Rocky is 6 foot 265 pounds, exceptionally strong, been a professional wrestler, so we both are not going to give up on this project. I'm on the back end outside the door trying to move it forward. Rock is on the front end, lifting and back pedaling, if we can actually move the damn thing. It's about 20 to 30 minutes, we got Rock's end to the high threshold at the 2nd door. I'm soaked with sweat, Rocky has probably worked off about 8 pounds already and now, Rock has to be able to lift his end high enough to get over the high threshold. I can't go around to help him now because, now that the piano has all the room but 1 ½ inches of clearance on the sides, it's a total jam. We continue to bust our balls over and over again and eventually he is able to get his end over and we move the piano till my end reaches the high threshold. Rock can't get out, he's pinned inside and it's up to me to get that last move over the threshold. It wasn't easy, but after a ton of grunting and more ball busting, it's finally inside. I was waiting for my Mother to drive up and say… "Sorry guys, we can't leave it there, you'll have to move it out." That nightmare didn't happen! We headed for a nice Steak house where we loaded up and had a story that would go down in our history books!

I grew up on Holden Street in the Highland Park district of southwest Seattle. Got there in 1940 when I was 2 years old, and left the day school let out in June 1954. Being an under sized runt in that ruff & tumble neighborhood during that period in my life, was not an easy thing to go through, but I survived it. My main goal as a kid was to get to the great West Seattle Hi School where I watched all the older kids go. September 1953 at the age of 15, being 5 foot three and 120 pounds I started my sophomore year at WSHS. The school year started out pretty low key, but there would be so many changes that would take place in my life, probably no other one year in my lifetime can compare. My immediate family was very small by comparison to the other people around me. Just my Grandpa, my Mother and me. My Mother had her own little business and she stayed away a lot. Grandpa had the neighborhood grocery store and had been there since before 1930. We lived in a shack behind the store that we called home.

I didn't realize it at the time, but later in life I knew that I was a liability at that point in my life, especially to my Mother. We got along sometimes, but not very much, and she stayed lost in her work, not the greatest Mother as a parent. It was right after I had started school that year that my body decided to grow. I would get home some nights after school, do my chores, lay down, and sleep right around till it was time to get up in the morning. I grew 5 inches in height in just 6 months and grew right out of my clothes. By March I was 5 foot eight, weighed 140 pounds, which was crazy for me, but I still had a long way to go physically.

Grandpa was the backbone of our little family, he had been the glue that kept everything going all those years. Nothing fancy and on top of that, Grandpa was a quiet man. My Mother would walk out the door to where ever she was going, just taking it for granted that Grandpa would be there to watch over me, but Grandpa had a full time job taking care of the store and it's probably a miracle something stupid never happened. I knew the price of everything in the store, I had worked behind the counter for years, I could jump in behind the counter just on instincts, wait on customers, run the till, no problem. A good portion of the customers knew me by my nick name and didn't hesitate to have me wait on them. We did have a little problem with the Beer though. My Grandpa sold gallons of Beer. His Beer trade was through the roof. I was warned a thousand times to keep my paws off the Beer, but… it was a power trip for me to have one of the customers come in during a busy period and say, "Hey Mick, grab me a full case of Old Style". I would jog into the walk in, grab the case, throw it on the counter and say, "$3.25". A done deal. Never got caught, but if a Seattle cop had seen that happen, it would have really hurt Grandpa's business. I thank the Lord nothing bad ever came of it.

It was in March of 1954, I had just turned 16 in January, and I knew Grandpa was having health problems for the first time in memory. The word Cancer was being thrown around and I knew he was making regular trips to the Doctor. He had a couple of the older ladies from the neighborhood that would come in and relieve him from time to time and it was happening more often now that his health had taken a change for the worse. On a particular morning in March, one of the older ladies was working in the store early. I could see Grandpa trying to get up out of his bed and get his clothes on. I was wise enough to tell he was in bad shape. He had this huge sore on his neck and it was draining. I got him dressed, called a Yellow Cab to come pick him up, they took Grandpa to the West Seattle General Hospital over in the junction. That would be the very last time Grandpa would ever see the inside of his house and store again. This day would also mark the beginning of so many changes that would happen in my life and everyone connected to me.

The next few months, a lot of it is foggy. One of the main things that would take place, my Mother could not face up to Grandpa being in his condition in the hospital. She didn't take responsibility of the store and, it was obvious she had more on her mind than even thinking about her son. She started drinking heavily and staying away for days at a time. I was pretty much left alone and then there would be the days she would show up, want to be the boss, argue about everything etc. etc. Take off and be gone again. During that period of time, I know I had the store open at least some of the time. It was 5 miles to school and the city bus stopped right across the street from the store picking up kids for **WSHS** at 7AM & 7:30AM. Earlier in the year I caught the early bus, but after all this was taking place, I would catch the 2nd bus and get to school 5 minutes before the bell rang. I tried to work things out with the older ladies to keep the store open some. If I got home from school and the store was operating, I might keep it open for a couple hours and run it myself. I was fixing my own meals, and of course, with my Mother gone a lot, I was staying there at night by myself. With Grandpa in the hospital at the junction, I could walk down there from the Hi School and visit him, and then catch the bus from there, home. After a while, they transferred him down to the Medical/Dental building in downtown Seattle. I would have to take the city bus on Saturday and go down to visit him. Usually stop at the YMCA while I was in town.

The last week before school let out, I was getting worn out staying at home alone. My Mother was staying gone all the time now. I started sleeping at nights a block away at Trainer's house. They knew the score and let me stay with them. I had been trying to line up some work over in Eastern Washington so I could get away. I got some potential promises but nothing definite. I turned all that into a little white lie. I told one of my friends at school that I had lined up some work. The day school would let out we could go over the mountains in his car and work for the summer. So... The day school let out, Jerry showed up at Trainer's house in his 41 Ford. Just minutes later, Mother shows up in a Yellow Cab, steps out drunk as a Lord, and starts a huge fight there on the street. All the neighbors were watching this horrible scene and it was my worst nightmare. Poor Jerry didn't know what to think of what was going on and I was totally embarrassed. Jerry turned his car around and left, I would never see him again until I saw him at a funeral 44 years later for his best friend Larry.

I had 19 bucks in my wallet and my bag was packed. I caught the bus down to the King Street Station. Bought a ticket to Pasco, Washington even though the train didn't leave till about 11PM. I rode the train all night. I remember the Porter bringing me 2 ham sandwiches. Those sandwiches hit the spot and for some unknown reason, that stayed etched in my brain forever. I pulled into Pasco at 5AM and walked to where my Dad lived alone. His wife Bertha, had passed away just a year earlier from a heart attack. I rang the bell, he answered the door, and he was getting ready for work at the Hanford Atomic plant in Richland. We hadn't seen each other for a year, I explained briefly what was going on. He went to work, I went to bed and slept. When he got home that evening, we had a long talk and I told him I was not going back to live with my Mother. He was easy to talk to, he said I could stay there and we got along fine. My Mother would eventually find out from him I was there, and what my feelings were. I found part-time jobs to work, made new friends, for the first time in a long, long time, I was actually living like a normal person should. Grandpa was on my mind a lot, but he was in the hospital and I knew that was the best I could do for him no matter where I was. Now that I'm decades older, I always wish I could have been in a position to do more for Grandpa, but I wasn't.

Been with my Dad for 2 months now and things seem to be going along good. I was making a little money with the small jobs I was doing and living in a small town like Pasco in 1954 was a lot of fun for me. Got to know the usher at the theatre, he would let my friends and I in after 10 at night. Overlies Pool Hall was always a neat place to be. I would get free pool for racking tables for the old Vets. They had a real malt shop where teen agers congregate, and I was able to meet girls that were a little different than big city girls. My Mother called my Dad to let me know Grandpa didn't have long to live. I caught the train, it left about 11PM and I rode all night to Seattle. I wanted to see Grandpa, but was dragging my feet knowing I would have to deal with my Mother. I was in town, but Grandpa died that morning before I was able to see him. It was a blow to the gut, so I finally met up with my Mother. She wasn't drinking, she was in a total meltdown, a continuous crying jag. She was living in a rental house just north of U Dub. She bought me a sport coat and shirt to wear to the funeral. I stayed in town for about 3 days. Gus Trainer and I moved a lot of things out of the store into storage. After the funeral, I caught the next train to Pasco.

It was only about 3 weeks now, and school would be starting again. I had already assumed I would be staying with my Dad and going to Pasco High. My Dad and I sat down for a long talk. We were able to converse in a good way and that is when he told me

I would have to go back to Seattle and live with my Mother. He said he just wasn't equipped to work, and see me through school. I told him I would not live with my Mother. He and I talked about a compromise. There was this school in Lacey, near Olympia, I could live there and go to school. I said I would go, and he said he would talk with my Mother. She agreed, so, the next step was to get the permission to apply for admission. I met up with my Mother the day school was to start. We drove down to Olympia and I was admitted to the school that evening. It was a real strange feeling. I didn't know a soul there and I didn't hardly know anything about the school. More big time re-adjustments were about to take place.

I wound up staying at St Martins for 2 years and graduated. Another very sad thing would take place just shortly after I had been there in the early fall of 1954. My Dad collapsed on the job at Hanford, they put him in the Walla Walla Veterans hospital. My Mother came down to school on a Saturday, picked me up and we drove to Walla Walla to visit my Dad. It would be the last time I would ever see him alive. He was dying of Kidney Cancer. Served in 2 World Wars and would die at the age of 57 years old. He gave my Mother his 40 Buick and his steamer trunk full of clothes. We had two cars to drive back to Seattle and I did part of the driving, and then back to school. Dad would die in March 1955. His body was transported to a V A cemetery in southern California. I made my first airplane flight to his funeral. It had been a really rough year, and I had to man up a lot and keep going forward. St Martins was a big stabilizing force in my life, even though I didn't realize it at the time. Even though I wasn't living with my Mother, we were getting along a little better. There should be better days ahead.

A couple days after graduation, I got a tip about working on a fishing boat at Point Roberts for the summer. I drove to Bellingham to meet with Mister Halgair Dahl about the job. We talked for about 30 minutes and he was sizing me up all this time. I was 6 foot tall and pushing 160 pounds, not one ounce of fat. When the conversation was about to end, he said, "Well… you look like you might be able to handle the job. Do you have two friends in pretty

The Cool Apple Express

good shape that might want to work for the summer?" I told him I was pretty sure I could get 2, but they went to public school and didn't get out till the 8th. "OK, you and your two friends be at the old cannery at Point Roberts on the 10th ready to work. Have good hip boots; a bucket hat, and Polaroid glasses to wear."

When I got back down to Seattle I knew just who I was going to ask if they wanted to work. My buddy Bill, who was graduating from Lincoln, and Tom, who was graduating from West Seattle. Bill was ready to go, couldn't wait. Tom was a way different story. He was all charged up and ready to go, but... his Mother hated me, his Dad was O K with it, but his Mother was a fanatic. She despised the fact Tom would associate with me primarily due to the fact I didn't live in a structured family. I came from a broken home. She always looked down her nose at me. Tom would tell me, "My Mother says you're a bad influence on me." He and I would joke around with that phrase for years way into adulthood. She thought I would take Tom up there and we were going to rob banks, etc. etc. She finally gave in, it wasn't easy.

On the 9th of June we headed up to Point Roberts in my 47 DeSoto. It was a fun little trip going up and we had a great time. I honestly believe that was the first time in his entire life that Tom was allowed to sleep in a bed outside of his house. He was going nuts with all this freedom he was having for the first time in his life. It's a good thing we were having fun 'cause that Norwegian had plans to work our asses off, and he did. To put it into a nutshell, that was probably the greatest summer of my entire life. We worked hard, ate good, had beautiful weather, and as a caveat, we had lots of Canadian girls just down the road at the resort. The Canadian girls liked us a lot, and we did have a little fun there when there was time. Halgair Dahl, the boss, would try to discourage us from going down where the girls were at, he wanted us to conserve all our energy for work. He didn't care if we were playing tackle football against the other boats, with no pads of course, on the sand spit, when we had slack low tides. The Canadian guys didn't like us at all, but who gives a damn about that? When Labor Day week-end came, Tom & me packed our bags and headed down to Seattle. Bill had worked out a deal to stay up there for one more month before he started school at U Dub. The day after Labor Day, I signed my name on the dotted line and was off into the U S Air Force for 4 years. Except for two trips home on leave, and a short trip after I was discharged, I stayed gone from Seattle for 9 years before I would return to live there again. It would actually be one of those strange series of events that pop up in my life from time to time that changes everything and I would wind up back home on the first of June 1965.

Back in Seattle to live for the next 40 years

Leaving Texas, where I lived, and coming back to Seattle was not a planned out thing, it was one of those things that just happened over a series of events that transpired in a matter of just a few days. I had been married with two kids, but my wife had filed for divorce little less than a year earlier. I had a good job, but when she decided to get the divorce, I was thrown out on my can. Slept in the back seat of my company car the first week till one of the guys I worked with let me sleep at his house till I could get a full pay check again. When I was thrown out, my Ex threw every document of mine in the dumpster. That was, H S diploma; Birth certificate; DD-214 from the Military and anything else she could find. It didn't seem important at the time because, there were so many things happening I completely forgot about those items.

Over the next several months I was adjusting to all the changes and trying to keep a normal footing. Early in 1965 the San Antonio Police Dept. was taking applications for new cadets at the academy and I was coaxed to apply, they accepted my application to take all the tests. I took all the tests and did real well. The final test would be on the Wednesday evening before Memorial Day weekend. On that evening we took the physical agility test and then had to run the 100 yard dash on asphalt in the dark. There were two plain clothes officers officiating all this and when they selected

The Cool Apple Express

the final group, they said "Let's huddle up". "OK... you guys have been selected to go to the academy. Here's your first assignment." And the first assignment was... bring in a laundry list of personal documents in 48 hours or you were totally disqualified. Well... that put me in a hell of a hole! I spent the next 2 days trying to get a hold of my Mother hoping she could help me out with some of this. I hadn't seen her in 3 years. We hadn't kept in touch that well. I tried several ways to contact her and nothing was working. Time was running out for me! On top of that, my Ex wanted me to keep the two girls on the week-end so her and her boyfriend could go out of town, I said sure. By the time the week-end arrived my whole effort with the SAPD had gone up in smoke. To add to all of this was, where was my Mother, was she still alive, what's up???

When I took the two girls to their grandma's and dropped them off, I made one of my world famous impulsive decisions. With my all-out effort that had gone up in smoke with the SAPD as a result of my wife throwing out all my documents, I felt totally screwed. On top of that, it had brought to my attention there must be something wrong back home with my Mother. My mind had made a big shift, and now it was important for me to get answers. Everything meaningful to me had been taken away from me at every turn and now it was my duty to find out about the condition of my Mother. I took the company car down to NABISCO and parked it in front of the office, put the key in the mail slot, and told them to deposit my check in the bank. I grabbed a batch of important clothes, threw them over my shoulder, had a friend of mine's Dad set me out on the high way, and I hitchhiked to Seattle. It was Sunday evening the 29th of May 1965 when I left. I got into downtown Seattle on the first of June, Wednesday night and caught a cab out to my Mother's house. It was real late but there was a dim light on inside. I rang the doorbell. The door opened, my Mother looked at me and turned white as a ghost. She had been in the spin & dry (alcoholic re-hab). Once it set in, she was real happy to see me. At least I could finally relax, and I did. That was the beginning of the next 40 years of my life before I would eventually move back to Texas.

One of the things that would change for the good from that point was, I was a fairly mature 27 year old by then. I had taken a share of my lumps, with the divorce and other bad luck. It seems like that kind of stuff builds more character than having things go easy for you. The same would be said for my Mother. We would finally build a positive bond between the two of us that we had never had before. Believe me, it was far from perfect, she would always have her periods of drinking that would shake up the system. For the most part though, we would have a good relationship as Mother and son, and the parental love I should have had for my Mother when I was growing up, it finally came to the surface, we had a loving relationship the rest of her life.

WORKING MY WAY INTO TRUCKING

After about 3 or 4 days of relaxing and unwinding from the hectic week I left behind, and the long 2400 mile hitchhiking venture from San Antonio, Texas to Seattle, Washington, it was time to look for a job if I was going to stay put now. I met up with an old friend of mine, Dick Lee, I hadn't seen in years. He had a roofing company and I would work for him 1 or 2 days a week, for walking around money while I was trying to find a full time job for myself. I was hitting the bricks pretty good going after anything I figured I could handle. I have to talk about the attempt to go to work for the Boeing Co.

    I went to Boeing an applied for work. They interviewed me, told me I could go to work as a pattern maker full time but, I first had to have some basic introduction and training at a specific location. I said sure, where do I go and what do I do. They sent me over to Franklin-Pierce High School in Tacoma. I was well groomed like I always am, drove down to the High school and followed the instructions I was told. I'd never been there before, so when I arrived at that location, I looked for the area that I was supposed to report to. I walked into this room, a man was standing there alone, I asked him if I was at the right place and told him who I was and why I was there. This guy lit into me like some drill sergeant the first ten minutes of boot camp. It was like I walked into a trap and it was sprung. This went on for only a couple minutes and I already knew I was outta there. I don't exactly remember what my parting words were, but they were pretty formidable. I never ever had any desire to go to work for Boeing from that moment forward. I might surprise myself decades later, but Boeing was not for me, not after this.

I had only been in Seattle a couple of weeks and I was out in a bar in Lynwood one night. I looked in the phone book to see if Hannan's were listed. Sure enough, I called the number. They answered and I asked for Rocky. When Rocky answered the phone and I said who I was he was almost speechless, and that's saying something. He came down to the bar and met up with me. That was a big time moment! We hadn't seen each other in about 18 years at that point. He was my best friend on Holden Street when we were small, and it was pretty euphoric to get together again. We have that world famous picture of Rocky & me taken on Holden Street in front of the store in the fall of 1944. That was a classic photo in my family and his. Helmet liner, M-1 training rifle and ready to protect the neighborhood. He had moved out to Alderwood-Manor sometime around 1948 and even though I saw his Mother one time, I didn't get to see him. My Mother & his were bonded like sisters and he and I were the same.

He was driving a brand new 1965 Autocar dump truck and I started coming out and meeting him a lot and riding along. I was liking this and thought this is something I would like to do. Rocky was a really accomplished driver, his Dad had him driving sidesaddle when he was 16 years old. He took a tanker over Snoqualmie Pass alone when he was only 18 years old. This particular unit had a 5X4 transmission, that's 20 forward gears. He put me in behind the wheel a few times but, it was just a little overwhelming at the time. I wanted to find a way to learn, a way where not so much was thrown at you at once. I would find out that it wasn't something that would happen overnight, it was going to take a while. It wasn't long after I had been riding with Rock, and he met up with a friend that ran a crew on a construction job. He wanted Rocky to come out and work for him, Rocky said, "no, but I have a friend looking for a job." Next thing I knew, I was over in Bellevue working on a sewer main job that would last for one year.

There wasn't anything fancy about what I was doing. I was basically a grunt with a shovel. I had to join the Laborer's Union, the wages were real good for the time period, my appetite went through the roof. I was in real good shape in those days but, if you have not been doing hard labor, your body has to adapt just like training for any sport. To keep your body moving steadily for 8 hours, less a half for lunch, took me about 2 weeks to hit a groove I was comfortable with. After that, I could cruise with the regular guys and then some, long as I had plenty to eat.

I worked that job for almost a year and then there was a short layoff till they opened up a job in Normandy Park that was another year, almost. By this time, most of the co-workers are bonded, and pretty friendly with one another. Every time I got the chance, I would jump into one of the dump trucks and dink around. The two we had on the job were 10 yarders, and pretty well worn. Never the less, I wanted to get the feel, try to learn little things on my own and log a little time for any kind of experience.

When I got laid off the Normandy Park job, it coincided with trying to help my Mother get some bums out of the store, that she had allowed to stay in there too long, not paying any rent. She still had the reins on grandpa's store, and over the years had different people leasing it, to run it. She pretty much kept her head in the sand with the store, concentrating on her little business, hoping they would send in the checks. The latest batch of bums were 6 months behind in their rent. After my going out there when they were 3 months behind, and getting a promise to pay, now it was time to throw them out. I checked to find out where I stood legally, and I was in good shape to give them the boot. I threw them out, confiscated their equipment, which I was allowed to do, and ran the store by myself for about 4 months. Running the store was not something I wanted to do for very long. It was the winter of 66/67, and for the very short term, I had to get a stock loan, and, diligently went about my business. I had left that neighborhood for good in 1954, and being back in the store every day for a while was kind of fun in a way, seeing a few people from the past I hadn't seen since I was a kid. As an adult at that time and place, I learned something that I had never been told as a little boy kid. There were people telling me different things about my grandpa. The one thing that was so profound to me was, how grandpa would trade out certain store bought goods with people in the neighborhood that would bring in their home canned goods during the Great Depression. It was a way of helping out people that just didn't have the money to buy, and the only way they could get the goods was to trade. Pretty enlightening stuff to me.

Gus Trainer, who had family connections for years, lived one block away from the store. Now that I was in the neighborhood, he was coming around pretty regular. He expressed to me many times he would be interested in taking over the store and running it himself. So… I had my Mother's attorney set up a contract that I help to write up. Gus was pretty much in agreement with it, and, Gus took over the operation of the store and I moved completely out. My step Dad, for only a couple of years, my Mothers 2nd and last husband, had been good friends with Gus, when they served in the Army during WWII, so Mom & Gus were not strangers. I got the store thing straightened out, it would be an asset again, and hopefully my Mother would be happy now, and I would have the Grocery store in my rear view mirror. I went immediately to work on a little construction job, but it only lasted a few weeks and then I was on to something else. I managed to stay fairly busy working this and that, also trying to get some sidesaddle time riding with Rocky and 1967 seemed to be a Generic year, pretty unexciting, and then I landed my first job at an actual trucking company, ONC. But Wait! There's More!

That sounds all nice and sanitary, going back to the old neighborhood and running the store for 4 months. It was except, in

The Cool Apple Express

my life you "never know what lurks right around the corner". I was real busy all the time I was out at the store. The small house in back of the store, where I had been raised 'til I was 16, had no furniture. I brought out a couple chairs, and put an old bed in Grandpa's bed room. I had an old T V set back in what we use to call the living room, it was football season and I could watch the games when it was slow. So... I had to wait the first 2 months to be OK'd for a liquor license to sell beer & wine. That was the way that store would make a profit. It was amazing how much beer you would sell on a fri or sat night. I had gotten the license finally after waiting the 2 months and was finally making a profit, and boy, it was busy at times selling all that beer.

I had just had the liquor license for a short time and then, on a Saturday afternoon, when I was real busy, through the door staggers this drunk warhoop female with a half full stubbie of beer in her hand. I stopped her in her tracks and told her, "You cannot come into this store with an open bottle of beer in your hand"! I ushered her out the door and on to the sidewalk, came back in and continued waiting on a busy crowd of people. A few minutes later this drunk warhoop comes back in the door with the beer in her hand and is working her way farther into the store this time. By the time I got to her, I pushed her through the swinging door, through the kitchen and into the living room. Back in the living room were 2 kids from up the street. Their family was poor, they didn't have a T V, and I would let them watch the one I had in the living room. I told them to keep an eye on her till I could get free and find a way to get rid of her. The last thing I needed was this drunk to get caught in the store with the beer, and a cop comes walking in.

It took a little while, and the store crowd finally died down. I Hi-tailed it to the living room and she was passed out on the floor. I looked through her purse for some I D. I found a prominent name and phone number. Called the number and this guy answered the phone. Asked him if he knew the woman. He said he knew her well. I explained the situation and asked him if he could come and get her. He said, "I'll be right there", and he was. He got there in about 20 minutes, parked his little sports car in front. After I met him, I threw the woman over my shoulder, the dress she had on flopped over her head and her beaver stuck out like a Star on a Christmas tree. The 2 young kids followed me out to the car where I placed the woman in the passenger seat. The 2 boys, 12 & 15 years old, had eyes as big as silver dollars and I didn't know it at the time, it was real important for me they were there.

The rest of the week-end was quiet after that, and I figured that story was over and done. A few laughs, a few big eyes from the boys up the street... all done!

Not long after I had opened the store on Monday morning, met the vendors, early customers, and things got real quiet. This guy walks through the door and asked me if I had found a wallet. I said, "No, I hadn't found any wallet. If I do, I definitely will let you know". The guy wasn't threatening at all, in the beginning and then... he cut loose with a statement that, "my wife said you had sex with her and took $180 out of her wallet, and I'm going to sue you!" He backed out the door pretty fast, got into his car and pulled out. I'm blind-sided again! He made a couple circles around the store and drove off. Later that afternoon he circled the store again in his car. I had called down to my friend Gus Trainer earlier about the whole thing and when the guy showed up again, he brought me down his 45, and I kept it with me. I had no idea what this crazy was going to do next.

Next morning I was contacted by an Officer with Seattle P D. He wanted me downtown to talk about the incident. I went to a downtown precinct and went into one of those rooms you see on Law & Order. The guy started questioning me and told me, the woman had said she had sex with me all day and I took $180 from her wallet and she was charging me with rape. The Cop told me I had to get an attorney, it was a 20 year trip to the Walls if I was convicted of rape. I had seen this movie several times by 1966, I was 28 years old and now it was actually happening to me. I had never had an attorney in Seattle up to this time in my life. My Mother had a family attorney she had used for years. I explained the situation, maybe she could talk to her attorney and he could tell me what to do.

Mom's attorney referred me to another attorney that handled that kind of situation. The first words out of that attorneys mouth was, "I hope you know, if you are convicted, you will get 20 years in prison". I had to put up a $100 retainer to protect myself over a Big Lie! The next time I met with the Police Officer he told me, "The District Attorney is dropping the case against you. The woman has changed her story 3 times already, you are off the hook." I don't have to say loud and clear, I was relieved, but… it happened! Also, one thing that definitely worked in my favor was, the two boys from up the street that I let watch T V. The fact they were prepared to tell the exact story I did, and the cops knew it. I think they really knew all along it was a big scam, but it leaves a lasting impression on your mind. One hundred dollars in 1966 was still a lot of money down the tube! The woman pointed the finger at me; I had to prove my innocence. In the end, she was not believable but no charges against her for lying. Life goes on.

Old Nasty Crack

My first job as a Teamster. I had gone down to ONC and talked to a boss, Pat Combs, about going to work there. I thought I would get a job driving a solo rig in town, that was the real appeal to me. He did hire me, but I was 3:00 PM Dock. More grunt work. After I got hired, I was under the impression you worked on the dock and then they would bump you to a truck and off the dock. So… I'm used to hard work, I run my motor at full tilt and show them what I can do. If I saw someone working hard, I would just work harder. By 6:00 PM the dock was one huge pile of freight going every direction. They put me loading the Tri-Cities trailers and I would load out 2½ to 3 trailers a night. So, many nights I would be the last one off the dock and wind up working a 12 hour shift. The Line Driver that pulled the Tri-Cities run was Jim Jamerson, and he would constantly come in early, come by the trailers, and always say, "Load that front trailer heavy!" So I did! In fact… one night I actually over did it.

I had a bunch of barrels that weighed 5 or 6 hundred pounds a piece. I got the barrel truck and started wheeling them up in the front of the trailer. I had about 15 barrels in there and I came in with one more… the nose goes down and the rear comes up. Scared the shit outta me! They ran a bunch of guys onto the back of the trailer, and I wheeled out a few barrels. No damage except the ego, I guess. Later on it could be a subject for a few laughs. Little did I know in 1967 that, Jim Jamerson, the Line Driver, would enter into a business deal with me in 1973. That's for another chapter.

The job at ONC, while I was there, was pretty routine stuff. It was pretty hard work, but I had worked a lot harder. To try to conger up anything more exciting to say about it would be laughable, but I did have one personal episode that happened off the job I'm about to tell you. One Friday night I actually finished up in 8 hours, which was rare. I was really tired, but I got away for a little recreation. The hours I did work were not conducive to getting out and partying much, and I was able to get in on a little of this on a Friday night. I wound up in a bar with a lot of action going on. I met up with this single female and we did the normal things, dance, drink, and talk, get acquainted. After a few hours we went to her apartment. We had carnal recreation all night, and for a guy that hadn't been getting much, it was about time. I wasn't that impressed with the woman, and she could have felt the same about me. The next day was one of those gloomy, dark, rainy late fall days. We laid around all day, and then I said, "I'll call this guy that works with me and maybe we can meet up at the Circle Tavern, have a few beers and socialize."

When I think back in time I couldn't tell you why I came up with that idea. I guess it had to do with stopping off at that particular tavern a few of the times that I got off early enough to have a beer or two with Steve, the guy that loaded trailers in the same area I did. I called Steve, never had before, and asked him if he wanted to go down to the Circle Tavern, maybe bring

The Cool Apple Express

a girlfriend, and he was game. I thought he was going to bring a woman companion with him, but when we arrived, he was already there, alone. The place was full of people, lots of single women, and any guy shouldn't have a problem getting hooked up. We were in a booth for a while, I danced a few dances with the woman I was with, Steve didn't ask any woman in the Tavern to dance, and I wasn't concerned at that time what he was doing. I got up to go to the restroom and was gone less than 5 minutes. When I got back, Steve was dancing with the woman I had come in with. At that moment, it still didn't register that anything might be wrong, I felt it was pretty innocent. But wait! There's more! I had been sitting down for just a few minutes, and I saw the table shaking, I reached under the table, and this Steve had his hand gripped with my date. I looked Steve straight in the eyes, and said "OUTSIDE!" I headed for the front door and got into the parking lot. Steve came out the door behind me and when we came face to face I blasted him one solid shot straight to the face. I poleaxed him. Shortly, the two uniformed Sheriff bouncers were on top of me pulling me off him. One guy was pretty big and he got me into a Full Nelson. He had me standing up facing the front door while he had me in the hold, all the time saying if I struggled I was going to jail. I didn't push it! It was at that moment, the woman I was with was standing in the doorway yelling, "He has the keys to my Thunderbird!" The Sheriff turned me loose and told me to give her the keys. I reached into my pocket and threw the keys at her. The two Sheriffs were actually pretty decent under the circumstances. They had a job to do. They said anymore fighting and we were going to jail, and we couldn't come back into the tavern. Steve, was finished, he had no fight left in him anyway. After a few minutes, I asked one of the Sheriff's if I could use the phone to get me a ride, I wasn't going to cause any trouble. He let me in, I called my longtime friend Tommy, Tom came down and picked me up.

The following Monday, not long after I had gotten to work, Steve arrived at my trailer. He said to me, "If I had known ahead of time you were going to punch me, things could have been different."

I SAID TO HIM. "WHAT IN THE HELL DO YOU THINK I INVITED YOU OUTSIDE FOR?" "We can go over there in the yard, between those two trailers, nobody is watching, and you can have a second chance." "Oh no, I don't want to go through that again!" I let it go there and I would see Steve from time to time over the years long after I left ONC. We crossed paths in the trucking business, he eventually became a driver too. It always intrigued me though, what was he thinking that night at the Tavern. Did he think that I would just sit there like a stooge while he was picking up on the woman I came in with? I guess in his own little mind he didn't have any respect for me. And the woman too? What the hell was she thinking? I had been gone less than 5 minutes, and somehow, 2 strangers built this immediate bond? Never made sense to me.

My longtime drinking buddy Bob, from construction, dropped by to see me, he told me they were working a job out in Edmonds, and if I wanted to come back to work for John again, the job was available. It was awful inviting, getting back on day shift again and being able to party at night again instead of working. I didn't hate things at ONC, but I was impatient about getting off the dock and getting on the trucks. So,…one evening, I punched out for lunch at 7:00PM and when I was eating my meal, I made the impulsive decision to get into my car, drive home, go to bed, and get up the next morning, go see John out in Edmonds about going to work, and I did. I sure wish I would have bowed out with a little more class than that. ONC deserved better. They were not a crummy place to work, but I am human and didn't always do everything right.

It's January now, cold, several inches of snow on the ground, and I'm out in Edmonds mucking around in the ground, back working with the old gang. It felt good at the time, we all got along pretty well. Bobby was telling me about the neat cocktail lounge across the street at the Chopsticks. The Chopsticks had this absolutely beautiful female bartender and fantastic food. We spent way too much time in there after hours. We felt we worked real hard during the day, and we could play hard afterwards, and we did.

I not only belonged to the Laborer's Union, I also belonged to the Teamster's too, so every time I got the chance, I would get into one of the dump trucks and drive. We finished up that job in April and I got laid off again. I didn't care, I was looking for a little break in the action.

There are certain things in life that I think are so funny they never leave my memory. I will get recall from them all through life and laugh all over again when I'm thinking about them. For some reason I have no answer for, I had a talent for leap frogging parking meters. I think I started doing it in High School sometime, and it was one of those things I could master real easily and become a pro at. Be downtown drinking in a bar with friends, get outside and start leap frogging parking meters, go through the cross walk and resume the whole line of them on the next block. So... one night, my buddy Bobby and I are out drinking after work in some bar somewhere. Bobby was not real short, but he was shorter than me. Bobby was stocky, and strong, he was no wimp. We exit the bar onto the street and I immediately start leap frogging a line of parking meters. I know Bobby had never tried it before. He had seen me do it, but I never coaxed him to try it. It was kinda my private thing and I would just do it. Well... I guess Bobby decided in his mind at that moment he was game to engage in Mike's sport and he was going to give it a shot. I heard him back there and looked over my left shoulder as he was making his first attempt. It wasn't working for him and I guess on about that third attempt, he got up high enough to almost ruin himself and let out this loud roar of pain. He was able to crash to the concrete, writhing in pain, and letting me know he wasn't having any fun at that moment. It was funnier than hell. Bobby gave up leap frogging parking meters for good!

My first real driving job and a great place to work

After a few days of goofing off, I decided I better stop into the Employment office to see if they had anything worthwhile, and to see about signing up for un-employment while I was there. I was slicked down in a nice pair of slacks, shirt and low quarter shoes.

When I checked in at the un- employment section they asked me if I belonged to a Union. I told them I belonged to 2 Unions. The lady whipped out 2 slips and informed me that I had to go to both Unions and let them know I was available for work. If they didn't have any work, they would stamp the slips, I could bring them back and be able to sign up for un-employment.

Went to the Laborer's Union, they didn't have any work. Next stop the Teamster's, should have went there first, it was only one block away. At the Teamsters, they told me I had to go to the Hiring hall down on Spokane Street across from The Ole Dutchman café. When I went into the Hiring hall for the very first time in my life, there was about 25-30 guys in there. My instant impression was, "you got way too many guys ahead of you to think about going to work." Wrong! The dispatcher asked me a few generic questions, and then he said… "Do you wanna go to work?"…and I said… "Sure!" He made out this card and told me to go over to LASME (Los Angeles-Seattle Motor Express) and report to the dispatcher there, with the card. It wasn't that far away so I didn't get lost. The dispatcher there was a PRINCE! His name was Bob Dinsmore, and it would turn out for me anyway, he would be the very best dispatcher of my entire trucking career.

Bob took my card, gave me a brief critique, since I was brand new, and told me when I got in in the evening, they would cut me a check for that day's work. He handed me a clipboard with 30 bills on it, told me where the loaded truck was and said, "See ya!" I was dressed more like I was going out on a date than taking out a fully loaded truck with 30 stops, at 10:00 AM. Har Vee Go! Got my brain in gear and my motor goin, and I was truckin the streets of Seattle. It was about 5:30 in the evening and I had all the freight delivered except for 3 stops that were closed. They brought me into the dock. I don't remember if it was that night after work, or, if I went to the hiring hall the next morning, but they requested me back the next day, and I showed up. I had a real good feel for being there and it turned out that way too. After a couple days in a row of working there, one of the bosses came down to see me on the dock after I had gotten there in the morning. He was the notorious Bob

The Cool Apple Express

White, and he called me over in a pretty stern way. He asked me if I wanted to work full time. I said yes! He said, "OK… you will have an 8:30 AM start, and you will drive whatever whoopee run they give you. If it's slow in the morning when you get here, I want you to go out on the dock and help the guys unload the trailers without having to ask you. If you get in the evenings early, you will work on the dock either stripping trucks, or, loading trailers. "Sounds great to me!" And, so… I became what they call a 20%, which means, I'm so far below the seniority list, they can put me where ever they wanted. No complaints from me. This is probably not worth mentioning but, I found out later, while I was working at LASME, my, Mothers 2nd and last husband was married to Bob White's aunt.

Sometimes in your life, person, places or things, have a more profound affect on you then most other things. Working at LASME would be one of those rare things, and to this very day, I could almost write an entire book on all of the overall effect, of the many different things at LASME, that would have a big effect on my life.

There are 2 things in this life I can say that I definitely don't have to worry about being called. A kiss ass, or a whiner. Bob, the dispatcher and I, got along so well, only a kiss ass could envy me. It was all natural, and everything Bob wanted done, I would just go out and do it. He showed his appreciation to me by treating me like a man. That was great! After a little time had passed, I felt like I would work there forever. I should know better than that in my life, and I would be wrong, because, the changes that would take place there were way out of my hands.

There were so many things to talk about, but, a lot of it would sound like bragging, and a lot of it would get into my personal life, I'm not going to get into that. One of the best ways to describe it would be, working at LASME was excellent chemistry. I was only at LASME for one full year, and they did a merge. They merged with 3 other trucking companies which inflated the seniority list very large. I was at the rock bottom of the list. The move took place with the move to the state of the art terminal in Tukwilla. I was put on 4:00 O'clock dock, and it wasn't easy for me to take at the time.

Mike Hicks at LASME, 1968/69. It was real fun while it lasted.

After a couple of weeks in the new terminal, Bob, the dispatcher, got a call, they wanted a full time driver for semi at Olympic Foundry, and Bobby didn't hesitate. He called me at home and told me to come down and see him before I started my shift at work. He explained to me about the job, and if I wanted to go to work over there immediately, it would be OK. I went to the foundry and met up with Big Jack Rowlands. He looked exactly like Brian Donlevy from the movies, mostly in the 40's. After we talked some, he told me to hook up to a 40 foot flatbed trailer, and then, "I want you to back it clear around the foundry". And so... I hooked up, proceeded to back it around the foundry. Made it in one crack! There was everything imaginable piled up along the way, and to this day, I don't know how I kept from screwing it up. Couldn't have done a better job on my best day! When I came out the other side, Jack was there waiting for me. He had put a spotter some feet behind me to walk around and make sure I didn't knock a building down, or, something of that nature. I was relieved, and everyone was happy, Jack said I was hired, and my career at Olympic Foundry had just begun.

I really didn't want to leave LASME, I loved it there, but, the handwriting was on the wall for me. I was at the bottom of a seniority list that was obviously going to be chopped, and it was. The merge had changed everything, and with the motorized tram that moved the freight continuously, that was going to cut jobs in itself. I made the change to Olympic Foundry and actually was lucky to have a good paying teamster job to go to. I would drop by LASME a lot for a long time and still talk about LASME a lot to this day.

I was at Olympic Foundry for 1 ½ years, until the lights went out at Boeing in Nov. 1970. I did have one week vacation coming when they laid me off. They actually gave me 3 weeks' vacation, which they didn't have to do. Looking back, it was great to get that extra money at the time, because, the next several months would be very dire, and very bleak in Seattle. Boeing would lay off 80,000 people in a matter of weeks, and that wasn't even factoring in a 12 year Metro project that ended at exactly the same time. I was hauling a lot of castings, and pipe to a lot of those jobs, and a lot of those construction workers would get laid off too. I was having big time problems in a personal relationship at that time that involved a Baby I loved, and I was responsible for and needed to support, and did. I hustled like hell on a daily basis to work as much as I could and it worked pretty good for a little while. One week, I worked 5 days for 5 different trucking companies. Once it got close to Christmas there was nothing. I finally had to do that two full day chore of waiting in the un-employment line just to get into the building to sign up. I never gave up looking, but it was the worse I had ever seen in my adult life. I did talk to a guy in Houston, Texas that pretty much would hire me off the phone if I wanted to come down and work there. If I had been footloose like I was in the past, I'm sure I would have gone, but I had this brand new baby girl to think about and support, and when her Mother and I made a permanent split on New Year's eve, I had to stick it out for my relationship with the baby, and to make sure I got things legally right too.

FORBES: I have to bring up the story about Forbes, or, Mr. Forbes, however he was called. It involves one of the strange things that happened while I was working at Olympic Foundry. Forbes was known by the local truckers in Seattle as the "Freight Cop", that would be at least one of his names. His job as best as I could tell it was, to patrol the entire waterfront area and especially all around the industrial area, just south of downtown, looking for unusual loads; obvious violations; off the wall things drivers of trucks would be doing. You usually didn't see him but he saw you. I was only stopped by him 2 times. Once for going a little too fast down 4th. S in a semi but, there was a special time he stopped me when I was at the foundry. When he stopped me for going too fast, he just give me a lot of gas and told me to watch it. The time he stopped me when I was working for the foundry, he did me a hell of a favor.

At the foundry, my main job was to drive the single screw tractor that pulled either the 40 foot trailer or, one of the 28 foot flats, and usually the one with the prehistoric crane/hoist. I did a lot of grunt work too, but that was just part of the job. One morning when I came to work, they had this strange job for me. I was to take a ¾ ton pick-up out off Nickerson, over by Foss Tug and pick up a pond boat. A pond boat is used by some logging companies and in aquatic places where they have lots of logs staged in the water. They are made of steel and built to take a lot of abuse. The one I was to pick up had just been built, it was brand new. When I got there and looked at it sitting on the trailer, it sure looked to me that this pond boat was way too big and heavy to be pulled around by a ¾ ton pick-up. The thing weighed 8,000 pounds not to mention, sitting on that trailer it was over width.

It's not like me to refuse to do a job, or, complain, unless I thought it might be deadly. I figured I would take a route where I

The Cool Apple Express

could go pretty slow and not impede the traffic. I went out 15th W. so I could use the waterfront and work my way down to Lucille St., make a left over to Airport Way and into the foundry. I thought it might be a little rough but, it was a lot tougher than I could even imagine. By the time I got to the waterfront I couldn't be more uncomfortable. Along comes Forbes! He pulled me over, got out of his unit and walked over to my window. "What do you have here?" I looked at Forbes and figured this is one time you want to shoot straight from the hip if ever there was a time. I told Forbes, "I am actually glad you stopped me. I'm surprised I made it this far and this load is scaring the shit out of me." Forbes was asking a lot of questions and during that process I told him where I worked, what they expected me to do and that, I was just trying to get the job done. I told him the pond boat weighed 8,000 pounds and he almost croaked. He shut down the whole operation then and there, told Olympic Foundry they would have to get the right equipment over there to re-load and haul the pond boat away.

I was relieved. I wasn't bawled out but, I got this same sentence thrown at me and it was, "the guy that owns that pickup hauls pond boats all over the state." When I look back in time at that statement, it's a huge insult to my intelligence. I've hauled loads of all kinds all over the USA. As hilly and mountainous as Washington is, and the fact you would be driving on wet roads a lot of that time… never happen! That set up was a death trap for the driver and anyone near him. Forbes did the right thing!

When 1971 started out I was living on peanuts. Places where I had been getting a little part-time work didn't even want to look at me when I came nosing around. It was pretty, pretty bleak! I remember this one opportunity I thought, had come along. I was scheduled to take a student trip for an outfit called B-Line. No matter how old you are, when you get looked at for the first time from a trucking company, they call it a "student trip". It was a Union job and I had seen their trucks around all the time, but never had anything to do with them. I met their driver, Jim, at their yard in Tukwilla. It was real dark and rainy that night. We were to take a full flatbed load of rebar to Vantage near the Columbia River. The only seat in the cab, besides the driver's seat, was a wooden apple crate. I started out sitting on that. The engine was a 220 Cummins with a 4x3 transmission. The brownie was so worn out you had to hunt and peck for the holes. I don't know where we changed seats, but my performance stunk, to say the least. I was jamming the brownie, and of course, it is hard to be your best when you are in equipment for the first time and the stuff is worn and weathered. Fighting Mother nature on the mountain pass, and just trying to make a good thing out of, which for you, is a bad thing. Somewhere between Snoqualmie Pass and Rye Grass, Jim the driver took over and then… we top off Vantage (Rye Grass) and he puts it into "Georgia Overdrive". I thought I would shit that wooden apple crate full! Just in case you do not know what "Georgia Overdrive" is, I will explain. This particular tractor we were in was an early 60's model conventional Peterbilt. It had a 4X3 transmission, which, is 12 forward gears. So… in order to get into "Georgia Overdrive", you will always be going downhill, in the 12th hole, and then… you put the main box of the transmission into neutral.

We just drop off one of the longest pulls in the country, 11 miles, and he takes it out of gear and lets it roll. I had heard about this in trucking songs, but this is the first time I ever witnessed it in person. During the trip, Jim, the other driver, had been talking about a B-Line driver that had just lost his leg going down this hill. He had lost his air, I guess, tried to get it stopped on the bottom ramp before going across the river, and rolled it. Ironically, after I had finished the trip, a business agent from the Union contacted me, he wanted me to donate half of my check from the student trip to the driver that had lost his leg. I did! Not only that, I knew as soon as I got back I would never set foot inside a B-Line rig ever again. I found out B-Line was having a lot of trouble with the Union, and I could understand why. The kind of stuff you have to deal with during hard times. Around early April a few promising things started to take place. I was getting a little part-time stuff that looked like it might develop into full time. I stayed with it for awhile and then… my oldest and best friend Rocky was working behind the scenes trying to help me out. He saw first-hand what was going on in my personal life and he had an idea. Our mutual friend Craig Stewart had taken a job with Joe Penberthy, who had two trucks on with LITTLE AUDREY TRANSPORTATION running Seattle to Chicago. Rocky felt that Craig, our friend, could get me on driving there, and I would have a job and also be out of town away from the stresses of some heavy duty personal problems.

I actually knew Joe Penberthy real well as a kid growing up on Holden Street. He had come out from North Dakota during the winter of 1951, which was a cold and snowy winter for Seattle. He lived for awhile with the Trainers only a block away from me. Alice was his sister and Gus was his brother-in-law. He had a 1939 DeSoto coupe with the new sawdust snow tires. I use to ride around with him in his car a lot, I was only 13 going on 14. He went to work for LASME as a line driver and stayed there long enough to become #2 in seniority. He quit, bought a truck and put it on with LITTLE AUDREY. In the beginning, he wasn't going to let me drive for him. I was 33 years old and he still had this vision of me being that freckled face kid on Holden Street. He was really hard headed about it. A whole lot of talking by Craig finally caused him to change his mind and give in. Later on down the road things would change and I would have to run and hide from him, he constantly would bug me to drive for him, even when I was already working somewhere else.

Driving For Joe; Driving For Dascher; Lots Of Windshield Time

Craig and I headed out of Seattle with a load gong to the South Water Market in Chicago. I will admit I was a little nervous for awhile. I knew a lot was expected of me, I wanted to look good doing the job, especially in front of a friend. I also felt I had to prove to Joe I was up to the job since other people said I could do it. We had a pretty well used 68 Kenworth Cabover with a 280 Cummins engine; 4X4 transmission which is 16 forward gears.

Breaking it down, that's two transmissions; a 4 gear main box and 4 gear brownie (auxiliary). The brownie was well worn and easy to hang up for a guy that wasn't use to it. I kept hanging the brownie up and it was really pissing Craig off. He was about ready to kick me out of the cab in western Montana. We made a stop in Livingston Montana for chow, shower and fuel.

I was real down on myself and got myself into a deep trance and said I was going to drive out of there and do a hell of a lot better. We pulled out of Livingston and almost like a miracle, things for me were a whole lot better and I was starting to master that brownie. I did manage to make a wrong turn out near Spearfish Wyoming and Craig and I are still talking about that to this very day. It will never ever be lived down if he and I live to be 150! We got way out in eastern South Dakota somewhere and lost all our electrical power. We were off the side of the road trying to find the problem. Where the headliner met the top of the windshield, was a brocaded grill running full width of the cab. The wiring was loomed inside the grill, and the million miles of movement wore the insulation off the wire. We taped all the wire and like Magic, we had electricity again. But wait! There's more!

While we were sitting on top of the dash doing all of this, a pick-up truck pulled up in front of us and stopped. Two 16 year old chics in bikini's stepped out and walked under the windshield. Craig and I couldn't believe our eyes! They came over to the door and said," Can we give you guys a hand?" Craig and I were so excited at the time, I don't even remember what we said. I do know we didn't molest them. They stayed about 5 minutes, then left. Craig and I are still talking about that too! We were back on the road again. We got to Muscateen, Iowa, it was early in the morning. The fog was pea soup, we had an appointment in Chicago we had to keep, so we are trying like hell to make time and overcome the elements. We got to the Water market pretty close to the appointed time and unloaded our frozen freight by hand.

We laid over in Chicago that night and up early the next morning to re-load. Normally, we would dead head up to Madison,

The Cool Apple Express

Wisconsin and get a load of OSCAR MEYER meat, but Joe had us get a load of some kind of meat in Chicago. We loaded the trailer and then weighed to see if we were legal. Well... we were overweight on the front of the trailer and Craig made a decision. We would have to take a back route for several hundred miles to avoid the scales at Hudson, Wisconsin and a few other places, till we could get into Minnesota. All of this was new to me but I was adjusting pretty good now and was getting more comfortable with the equipment and everything else as time went by.

When it came time for me to drive it was at night and the weather was really turning to shit. Craig climbed into the bunk and I wanted to do a good job so that he could sleep, which he did. As the night wore on the weather got nastier. We were in a full blown thunder & lightening storm with trees being hit along the way. I kept the route he told me to stay on and just trucked away hoping the guy would get as much sleep as possible. Early in the morning at first light Craig got up and we were still whipping down the highway. The weather had eased off by now, and as far as I could tell, he didn't even know about the storm we had passed through. The rest of the way back to Seattle was pretty routine and things came out fine. Craig had told me at the beginning of the trip that he and another trucking friend were going to be full time driving partners when we got back. I would be making my next trip with Danny. I really learned a lot from Craig on that one trip. It was a little rough in the beginning, so much stuff was all new to me. It was really good for me to have made that trip with a real good driver like Craig, it paid off so much for me the rest of my entire trucking career.

In about a day and a half I got together with Danny and we headed to eastern Washington to load up apples for the south Water Market in Chicago. Danny was one of the biggest contrarians I have ever met in my life. This was the first time he had ever been first seat on a truck. He had been running 2nd seat forever with a guy called J C. J C was owned by Joe. By that I mean, he was a good and experienced driver and true to Joe and, would do anything Joe asked. J C would be one of those people that is always going to have a personal crisis of some kind in his life. If you came up upon him on any given day, he would be having a problem, probably personal in some way. The funny thing was, J C was Danny's hero, and now that Danny had a responsibility with a complete stranger like me, he didn't know how to act. I was new to this bunch and I had to take a back seat to a lot of things. Danny wasn't the greatest driver, but he was safe to run with and that is very important. It was a real struggle from the stand point of having to be in a cab with a guy for 6 days at a time and you had nothing in common. I made two complete trips with Danny and then I got a better opportunity.

Like I said, I was only with Danny for 2 trips, 2 weeks. It wouldn't matter what I would say, or do, Danny was going to take the opposite position or point of view. Strangely enough, the one controversial thing that did happen during those two trips was not personal. What happened was this. When you have a reefer trailer loaded with a product like apples, they will put what they call a Ryan Recorder in with the freight to record the inside temp of the trailer from Point A to Point B. When you arrive at the customer to unload, they have the opportunity to check and see if the freight has been kept at a proper temperature. We were taking a full load of apples and that trip usually takes about 42 hours. We brought the load into the famous South Water Market in Chicago. The Water market back in 1971 looked exactly like some place in a 3rd world country. If you have seen a movie scene, say in India, and they have this big open air market with a lot of stalls and crowded with people, that's the Water Market. You have to drive a tractor-trailer into an area like that and back it into a designated spot. Never enough room to move around. Loads from all over the U S would line up there to come in and unload. It was really something! So… on this day of our 2nd trip together, we got backed in to unload. There was about 3 guys there to unload which meant we didn't have to do the grunt work and that's kind of rare actually. I was standing by the trailer door when one of the men reached up to get the Ryan Recorder. He looked it over and said, "We can't

The Cool Apple Express

take this load, it's been running at 53 degrees, the load is no good." I looked over at Danny, and he was speechless… he was lost in space. I waited for him to respond and he never did. It was his responsibility in a situation like this and I didn't want to try to upstage him. Finally, I spoke up to the man with the Ryan Recorder and said to him, "I have a pulping thermometer, let's check the fruit because, I have been watching that refer gauge all the way out here and I'll bet that recorder is wrong." We opened a couple boxes and started checking the temps and they were perfect. It showed the refer had been keeping the fruit at about 37 degrees. They pulped several apples and all were the same. Problem solved, the guy said, "let's unload this trailer." We were bailed out but Danny wasn't about to say thanks, or, give in, so things stayed the same till we got back home.

After I had gotten back into Seattle from that 3rd trip, second one with Danny, I told Joe I was getting off the truck for now. The three weeks of solid driving Seattle-Chicago, it was like being in school, as far as furthering my education in Truck Driving II. The knowledge couldn't be replaced! This was not severing my relationship with Joe as far as trucking went. He and I would have an enduring relationship, in segments. It will be explained as time goes on.

Rocky knew I was back in town and I had only been back about 2 days when he called me. He told me to get over to the east side of the lake where he was working, he had gotten me a job driving belly-dump for Jack Dascher at Redmond Sand. I reminded Rocky I didn't have any belly-dump experience and of course he said, "Just get over here, you've got the job and you can ride with me today." He had a Kenworth conventional with a 350 Gimmy and a 4x4. I rode all day with him and sat in some and things went O K. Jack Dascher ran the trucks over there, I had heard all about him but I didn't know him yet. He use to like to get Rocky and his brother Bob along with a collection of other guys when he had some steady things going. There was lots of work, the wages were great, and I just kept my mouth shut and did what I was told.

The first day on the job worked out fine as I remember. They assigned me to a unit and everything came out O K. It always helps to get off to a good start for a whole lot of reasons. Almost the entire crew were all good guys, and it was easy to fall into the groove of working there.

After working there for a week, it was like I had been there for a long time. Little mechanical things happen to everybody working in that environment, but no major problems. After 3 weeks of my working there, a lot of us became part of a very busy job entailing lots of hours. A Longshoremans strike up in Canada had shut down an important supply of product for HOOKER Chemical in Tacoma. There was a mountain of rock salt paralyzed on the dock in Vancouver B C and they had to find a way to get it down to the Tacoma plant. Redmond Sand said they could do it with belly-dumps, and so… we started a daisy-chain of rigs running between Tacoma and Vancouver, BC.

Up in BC on the dock, they left a Cat 944 rubber tire loader with a 2 ½ yard bucket. If you didn't know how to run one you got a chance to learn because, there was no one there but you. You pulled up to the pile and loaded it yourself. No scales to weigh, so it was a guessing game. You wanted to haul a pay load, and you had to distribute the weight correctly because, there were two scales to go over on the way to Tacoma. It was a great job to be on. The work was routine. It was a 350 mile turn around, lots of windshield time. When you got to HOOKER Chemical on 11th street at the tide flats, you got a head of steam through the yard, tripped the gate switch, and in less than 10 seconds you were empty and on your way for another load.

It got to where they wanted us to do 2 turns a shift. If everything goes right, that's 700 miles, plus, whatever time it would take you to get in and load up. 7OO miles in one shift is a lot of honking. To put it in perspective, that would be the same distance from Seattle to Sacramento, California. The one big downside to this whole idea was, we had super single tires on all of the trailers. One of them babies blows out and you are down. We had no 2 ways, and of

The Cool Apple Express

course, cell phones were about 30 years into the future, so, you had to flag someone down just to get a call back to the yard. Everybody had flats, and everybody was on the shoulder for hours when they broke down.

There was a problem getting into the yard late at night because, the fence would be locked and guys were coming in at all hours, stuck outside the gate. I suggested we put a nail in the tree outside the gate and hang a key on it. This turned out to solve the problem and it worked real well. BUT WAIT! THERE'S MORE! On one particular night, I was coming in after putting in a 32 hour shift. I had been doing stuff like that on a regular basis by that time, and boy was I owly! It was good I was all by myself. I pulled my 68 Freightliner up near the fence, stopped and went over to the tree to get the key. No key! I looked all over the tree and on the ground, no key!

I scaled the fence, put my shoulder into the door of the shack, and popped it open. Got on the phone and called Jack Dascher. I told Jack the problem and asked him, "what do you want me to do now?" He said, "I'm in bed and I'm sure you will figure out what to do." I looked over at the Cat 966 loader sitting in the yard. I jumped up in it, started it and moved over to the gate near the lock. There was a big piece of chain threaded through the cyclone fence with the lock on it. I put one tooth on the bucket through a link of chain, put it in reverse, and it's amazing how fast an entire cyclone fence can hit the ground with that kind of power. I was hoping to only break the chain free but I got a whole lot more for my little effort. I parked the loader, drove in my rig and parked it, went home dead tired.

At about 5AM, the owner came to the yard, and was in shock! He called Dascher to tell him. Jack did not spill the beans! He said, "Someone must have broken in, did they steal anything?" Nothing was stolen and I was never given hell for it, but when Rocky found out, he told everyone in North America for years afterwards. For some reason, that was one of his favorite stories to tell.

UP IN PORT ANGELES

It was Labor Day 1971 and Jack Dascher asked me if I would go up to Port Angeles and work on a job for J E Work. Const. He picked me because, I was divorced, he figured it would be a lot easier to get a guy like me to go to an out of town job for a couple months, than to ask one of the married guys. No problem, but I had to get a belly dump up there and also get my car up there. I figured out the perfect plan. I had a good friend of mine that helped run a tire shop on Lake City Way. There were some of these young guys that use to hang out there, and I paid 2 of them to drive my Gold Gran Prix up there. One of them followed in their car, I lead in the belly dump and paid for the ferry tickets. It worked out good till I had to do it again when I made the reverse trip in November. We did it in the dark of Labor Day evening, all the cars coming back towards Seattle for the start of school and the end of summer, they were blinding us with their head lights. The first day I was in Port Angeles it was a ghost town with all the summer vacationers gone. I had a place to park my rig, but leave it to me to decide to stay at the best motel in town "Aggies Motel". I sure wish I would have looked around and found a place for half the price but not me. I would stay at Aggies the whole time I worked up there checking out on Friday mornings before going to work, and making reservations to stay the following week. Leave after work on Friday afternoons and drive down to Seattle.

It was kind of a neat little job. I didn't know a soul again when I arrived. There would be 4 drivers including me, 2 other lease drivers, and the truck boss that also drove, and he and I would become friends. They had set up a conveyor in a small pit next to the garbage dump. We were hauling screens (a form of crushed rock) to an area a little over a mile away, using the screens for the foundation of new roads that were going to be paved. Right out the shute, one of the chains on the gate dumper of my trailer broke and I had to get to a welder and get that taken care of. Never want to be an outsider like me and go into a job like this and not have it go absolutely perfect the very first day. First impression in this kind of thing can cast you immediately no matter how good you might be, but, this time would turn out O K, and once we got going, and for ever after on that job, everything would work out fine.

There was a driver there named Dick Taylor, and I met him for the first time. Dick and I had good chemistry, and we became friends. He owned his own truck and he rented this small rental while he was there, like I should have. We use to talk about everything. He was from Kirkland and had lived there for a long time. I had my Kirkland connections too, in the form of friends. I had coached Little League football there in 1966. My baby daughter's Mother had been raised there. We even went salmon fishing one after noon out by Ediz Hook. Dick was a little older than me and he knew some of the people I knew. I found out after I left that job that Dick had a stellar reputation for a few things. All good in my estimation. It made it nice to be able to make a friend with Dick because there wasn't a lot to do up there when work was over. The truck boss and I went to a party in Sequim one night, and also played catch with the football on a few occasions. He was able to stay with his aunt while he was there, and one evening when I dropped by, she answered the door, I asked her "can your nephew come out and play? "She thought that was funnier than hell, especially since she didn't know me from a bale of hay.

The Cool Apple Express

I had this knockout looking lady friend in Seattle, she wasn't solely mine, but I knew she liked me, and I knew when I made myself available, she would usually get together, so, when we were done on Friday afternoon, and I was free to travel, I would crank up that Palomino Gold Pontiac of mine, head for the ferry and to Seattle. I was 33 years old and the fire was burning.

I usually caught a ferry on Sunday evening, drive up the Penninsula to Port Angeles, get my room at Aggies, and sleep till 6, get to my rig and get it ready for the day. On a particular weekend, I was having a real enjoyable time with this particular lady, and I checked to see what time the first ferry left in the morning. They told me 3AM, so I decided I would stay back and give that a shot. Well... I caught the early ferry, and when I got off on the other side it was pitch black and super quiet. I was the only one on the road. I nailed it to the wood and was cruising along at about 80mph and then... an Elk, or Mule Deer stepped out in front of me... whewwwwwwww I went between him and the guard rail, did a 360 and dented my right front fender pretty good. I came to a complete stop to catch my breath. If he had doubled back, he would have decapitated me. I can fix the fender. I don't think my pants were full, but they should have been. My Grand Prix sat real low, and a sure death trap if the animal doubles back or goes thru the windshield. I hadn't slept, but I was wide awake, and when I arrived in P A, I wouldn't have any trouble staying awake that particular day. I found a guy up there that did the body work on the fender and spray painted it for me while I worked all week. The snows started falling on Hurricane Ridge in early November, and they shut the job down not long after that. It was a positive couple of months, I kind of hated to see things come to an end. I made a couple friends that I would see off and on for a long time. All was not lost.

By the time I got back to Seattle, things at Redmond Sand had really slowed down. It became apparent I was laid off even though no one officially told me so. I took this opportunity to rest and party a little, which at first was a nice break in the action. I drove down to San Bernardino, California and spent one week with a nurse I had been writing to. She would come home from work, give me a B12 shot every night and we spent a little time trying to enjoy each other's company. On the way back to Seattle I stopped at G I Joe's in Portland. They always had real good prices in those days. I found this real neat Formula I sports car, (kiddie size model) and it had a broken rear wheel. I made a deal with the store and scored a great price. When I got back home I went to the hardware store and bought two wheels a little bigger than the one that was broken. I put those two wheels on the back of that car and it gave it the neatest rake look you could imagine. Christmas was only a few weeks away and that sweet 1 ½ year old daughter of mine was going to get that great ride as a present.

1972

ALL OVER THE PLACE LIKE A FART IN A SKILLET

OF ALL THE YEARS I can think of, clear back to my youth, man… 1972 had so many different things going on I have to think extra hard to keep it all straight. Dascher had some people using the tractor I had been driving at Redmond Sand, making trips somewhere, I know he wasn't using me. I made a few trips for Joe to Chicago, and I think I was also taking some casual work for Trans-Con. It must have been around February and Dascher called me to go back on the Freightliner, he had a pal over in Seattle that had trucks hauling produce for Pacific Fruit and I guess he found a way to keep the Freightliner busy for a while. I knew who the guy was and I wasn't that wild about driving over there but it was still winter, and I kind of figured the truck would eventually get back over at Redmond Sand.

I started making these runs to the bay area with frozen food, and then picking up produce of all kinds in places like Lodi, Stockton, Sacramento, etc. Running it back to Seattle as fast as you can to be into Pacific Fruit by 6 AM. He didn't give a damn if you ever went to bed, they wanted you to keep the schedule no matter what. It was a brutal, brutal schedule, and I just would not take bennies. I did get into the habit of taking No-Doze, & coffee, and that stuff ate up my guts. One night I was in Eugene, dead ass tired, it was another 300 miles to Seattle. I didn't want to stop, so I forced down some more No-Doze & coffee and headed north. When I got to about Kelso, I hit this mini blizzard. It was snowing like a bat out of hell and watching those flakes coming down, as tired as I was, gave me vertigo, it had happened before. I was dizzier than Judy Holiday. I spotted this rest area just in time, pulled in and stopped. I got out and proceeded to run around my rig about 40 times. The cool air cleared things up some and I took a needed break for about 10 minutes.

Once I got going again I was doing a little better and also, the snow started dying down which made it a hell of a lot easier. I got to the rest area north bound at Federal Way, and I just had to pull in there and lay down before I ran off the road, I was spent. I don't know how long I was there, maybe 2 hours and then, there was this big pounding on the side of my cab. It was a Washington State Patrol cop giving me a batch of shit because I was in the area for rec vehicles and not trucks. It was so dark and wet, and I was so tired when I got in there, all I know is I was off the highway and the rig was locked up. I always thought that's what those do-gooder guys at the WSP wanted truckers to do when they were in the condition I was, but I guess that is all do-gooder talk. I got up, cranked it over, and headed out, back on I-5 for Pacific Fruit. Don't even remember if I got there by 6, but I do know it was early morning.

One time I was down in that northern California breadbasket of produce stopping at different produce sheds, picking up and putting together my backload to take up north. I had been parked in this loading area taking on whatever freight I was picking up there. There were a few of these young Mexican guys doing the work. I had walked away from my equipment and then I remembered I had to get up in the cab to pick up something. When I opened

The Cool Apple Express

the door and started to get into my cab, I saw this young Mexican guy looking through stuff near the sleeper. With my temperament, I might normally swing first and ask questions afterwards but, instead I asked him, "What are you doing in here?" He answers back, "Hey man... jew got any beans?" He was referring to bennies of course. I told him, "no man... I ain't got no beans." He climbed out of the cab and I looked around to see if anything was gone. Nothing was missing but this guy didn't know he had coined a phrase in my circle that would last for a while. I told Rocky the story and for a long time, that's how we would greet each other. "Hey man... jew got any beans?"

I had been doing this for about 6 weeks without any incidents and then one day, this stranger comes over to the cab of my tractor and says he was going to be taking over. That was a Sunday punch! I checked to see what in the hell was going on. They informed me, I could stay on the truck as a 2nd driver if I wanted, but they were going to put this guy in as the lead driver. I told them, just as soon as I could un-hook my radio and pull it out of the cab, I would be in my car driving out of the parking lot. I knew the guy that ran those trucks over there was two faced and this was all the proof I needed. Joe had run into me when I was over there one day and he warned me about that guy. He was 100% right on!

So after a few days to get that out of my mind I probably started mixing some trips for Joe with working out of the hiring hall, or over at Trans-Con. Time passed a little and then I got a call from this woman they called "Mrs. Rainbow". She along with her husband owned one CO 71 Peterbilt they were running mainly to the Twin Cities with apples to Red Owl Warehouses, and they had a steady back haul of Schmidt's beer out of St Paul to the Pacific Northwest. For an over the road haul, they don't get much better than that one. I had never heard of them but, they were having Earl Dean servicing their Pete. They wanted a driver to be first seat on the truck and Earl had given them my name. Mrs. Rainbow asked me if I would or could come to work for them and drive the Pete. I figured I could make at least one trip and if I didn't like it, get off, so I said I would.

When I got over to their house to talk about it, her husband Harry was there, and it was obvious the guy was an asshole. He was telling me what a great driver he was and blah blah blah etc. He had this neighbor friend named "Frenchy", and he told me Frenchy would be my driving partner. I assumed Frenchy knew how to drive, he didn't tell me he couldn't, and I was taking it all in. We went to eastern Washington to pick up a load of apples headed for the Twin Cities. I drove to the apple shed and we loaded up. After we got started, I figured I would let this Frenchy get behind the wheel and drive, it was a good place to start. I couldn't believe what I saw!!! How in the hell this Harry could send a guy like this out with somebody new like me expecting he was supposed to know how to drive. I told the guy immediately, "you do not know how to drive, what in the hell are you doing here?" He began to tell me that he had made one trip already with Harry, and Harry had let him drive and said he was getting better.

It's 1800 miles to the Twin Cities not to mention the physical work of loading the trailer. I got over Look-out Pass into Montana and I was getting tired. I thought after we got by Superior Montana, I might be able to turn this guy loose long enough to grab a quick nap. I got him back into the driver's seat and told him to relax and do the best he can. I climbed into the bunk and away we went, not very far though. Frenchy was tearing up the transmission, I just couldn't let him drive. I got the hell up and had him pull over. We tried this once or twice more on the way to Minnesota with the same results. We made it into Minneapolis and I was burned out, but we got the load off. There were two nice motels where we could stay at and I picked the one where everyone usually stayed. This is where it gets fun for awhile. We were in the restaurant & lounge, eating and having a few drinks. I was about to go to the room, take a shower and crash. I told Frenchy, he better finish up, get in the sack, we were getting up early to get down to the Schmidt's Brewery and get loaded. But Wait! There's More! Frenchy tells me, "We are on our free time now. I'm not going to bed. We've made this trip out here and you can't tell me what I'm going to do. I'm going to party down here tonight." My voice box froze for a few seconds and then... I said, "If I had my way, I would have fired you onto a Greyhound bus in Spokane and sent your sorry ass back to Seattle. You cannot drive a lick, I cannot put you into the driver's seat, you will tear up our truck. I drove all the way out here and you say this is your free time? Tomorrow... when that truck is loaded and we are headed back. You are going to sit on the dog house and you are going to put your shifting hand on top of my hand and by the time we get back to Seattle you will know at least a little bit about the job you are being paid to do. Get your ass to bed shit head!"

Schmidt's Brewery was a classy place. If you could get down there in the morning and time it right, they would have your trailer loaded and ready to go about 11 AM. That coincided with the opening of the Rathskeller downstairs. Go into the Rathskeller and eat to your hearts content great food. They also had a cooler full of beer, the guy that was going into the sleeper on the way out could also have a few brewskies with his lunch. I loved it. Schmidt's would also give you one full case of beer more than the load, but if you could come up with a case of apples, that could easily turn into 5 cases. Don't get much better than that for places to load anywhere.

On the way back to Seattle, Mr. Frenchy had a huge attitude adjustment change. I had him up on the doghouse with his hand over my shifting hand and giving lessons like a professor. I let him drive a little, but very little. When we got closer to home he coped the plea to me. He told me that Harry couldn't hold a candle to my driving and acquired trucking knowledge, (thank you Rocky and Craig). He was finally sympathetic to my way of thinking about real trucking now. As soon as we got back I didn't hesitate to let Harry know he stiffed me by putting this guy with no trucking knowledge with me, and expecting me to make the trip thinking I had help. The truck was scheduled for some work with Earl, and during that week it was decided my friend Rocky was going to be my next driving partner. Boy are we gonna have fun now.

The week before I started driving for Mr. & Mrs. Rainbow, some other guy had made one trip to the Twin—Cities and back, and Earl was pretty sure he had burnt the top off one of the pistons. Nobody told me a thing till I got back and Earl was going to take the engine down and do an in frame type overhaul. Rocky was going to be my driving partner and he got all mentally involved and the whole next week, He & I were over at Earls while he was working on the engine. We were in coveralls trying to be helpful and get the truck in first class shape.

Just two days before we were to pull out and go over to eastern Washington and load apples we stopped off at John's (Petosa's) to have a few drinks and socialize, that was the major hangout of the day. Besides me, there was Rock's wife Kay, and one of Rock's longtime friends Dick Welch. After being in there for a while, Kay got bored & restless listening to all our B S and wanted to go some place else. Rock said, "OK, let's go down to the Owl Tavern." So, all 4 of us got in one car and drove down to the Owl. When we got out of the car at the far end of the parking lot, man… you could hear the band inside going full tilt with a whole lot of yelling and screaming. I had this gut feeling from the git go trouble was just around the corner. We got in and sat down at a table right in the middle and it was so loud in there you couldn't hear yourself talk. A biker club had pretty much taken over the bar and it was bedlam. We hadn't been sitting down 10 minutes and this biker guy grabs the mike, and wants everyone in the bar to toast so and so that's getting married. Rocky turns around and tells the guy "I'm not toastin!" The biker with the mike blurted out something at Rocky and Rocky told him to get outside. Rocky got up, I got up, we headed out the north door that was a side door, and came around south where the east door was the main door. When these guys started coming out he and I each grabbed one and started punching. About 16 bikers came out the main door and they all piled in on us. For awhile I was just fighting for my life. I don't know how many guys were on me, swinging Harley chains at me. One chain nailed me right on the forehead. It's when I heard this glass break that got my attention. I thought this gang of guys that had me down were going to cut my throat with a broken bottle. They had my arms completely enclosed, there was no way I could move them. I managed to raise myself off the ground with strength I didn't know I could muster, and look straight ahead with all these guys hanging on me and Dick Welch is right in my eye sight staring right at me. The look of fear on his face was priceless. I really didn't have the time to worry about that. He was a pretty good sized guy and he was frozen in his tracks. The bikers weren't messing with him, just me and Rock. I yelled at Dick to get these guys off me and he just starred in absolute fright. About that time I got nailed across the right shoulder with a chain.

It was about then, when we were so overwhelmed that the leader yelled out to let the guys up. When I looked over at Rock after I got standing, he was still on the ground. They had been whipping him with Harley chains, I wasn't able to see it with all I had to handle. I always remember this one young woman looking at me, I looked down and the bottom of my shirt was completely soaked with blood. About that time Rock says to me as these guys are preparing to mount up and get going, "Let's pick off the last two as they drive out of here," and so we did. They all did u-turns came back and piled on us again. This time I had a bunch of them giving me the boot with my face in the ground. Three car loads of Sheriffs pulled up but, they didn't get out of the cars. The action was still going on and I was looking up from the ground wondering what they were looking at and not making any moves to get out of their cars. I'm pretty sure, because they were way out numbered, they were playing it cautious to see if these guys would pull off with the sight of the 3 Sheriff cars. It did slow things down and then the sheriffs slowly exited their vehicles. Once I stood up, that same woman was looking at me in some kind of wonderment. The bikers were herding up again to move out. I saw the Sheriffs over there talking and milling around, but they weren't threatening anybody. I went back to the restroom to kind of clean up and then, that's when I saw what the young woman was looking at. One chain had hit me in the right corner of my forehead and it had bled all over my face. My face was completely covered in blood. The top of my shirt didn't look all that bad, but the bottom was totally soaked in my blood.

John had gotten word up at his restaurant what was going on and somehow got the keys to my 66 GTO convertible and drove down to the Owl just as things were winding down. They put Rocky and me in the car and drove back up to his restaurant. John closed the place and a bunch of us were back in the lounge till about 4 AM. They were cleaning up my wounds and tending to Rock's too. That story would be told a thousand times. Not by me, I didn't have to. Everybody in the area seemed to know about it and over the years, I heard so many versions of it from people that weren't even there. My friend Rocky passed away in 2007, we had a few exciting things to talk about in our time.

Two days after the Brawl at the Owl, Rocky & I are heading into eastern Washington to load up apples for the Twin-Cities. We're kind of scarred up some, but that's not gonna stop us. It was actually the first time we ever made sleeper runs together. We had a lot of fun and did a little work along the way. We only made two trips and he wanted off the truck. I made one more trip after he got off and then I got off. No hard feelings, I wasn't making that much money working there even though it was a great haul. I could do better being active out of the hiring hall till something better comes along. I had enough stuff to keep me busy and Joe was always there if I needed to work, or, if he needed me to make trips. So… 1972 kept on Truckin. Oh yeah… Rocky's long time buddy Dick Welch, the other guy that was with us at the Owl and watched, but didn't help. He dropped off the planet. According to Rocky, he never seen him again and there was a rumor, he had moved to Moses Lake and became a cop.

1973

LOTS OF DRIVING AND A FEW ODD ENCOUNTERS

It was shortly after the Christmas (1972) Holidays that I got a call from Joe Hester, and he wanted to know if I would run sleeper with him on his rig. Joe was a living trucking legend from the Greater Seattle area. I had met him for the first time just one year earlier. He had been a line driver for LASME, a driver and dispatcher for Lee & Eastes to name just a few. He had been running his own rig and just put it on with ONC Alfreight. Most everybody running there ran roll & rest, but he wanted to run sleeper. I had been making some trips for Joe Penberthy at Little Audrey and got off the truck for the Holidays, so I was wide open to take the job. I told Joe yes, I look forward to running with you, when do you want me to start?

It was only a couple days since he asked me to drive with him and he already had his trailer loaded for a trip to Los Angeles. I got into the cab and he said, "You can drive out." I got behind the wheel and he was immediately pleased with my driving and the way I handled his rig. Cab Over Petes were real popular at that time. That's what he had, and that's what I had been driving for Joe Penberthy exclusively. They had 350 Cummins; 13 speed; air ride suspension; jake brake, all the usual good stuff. Joe and I got along great and most everything we were doing was pretty routine. I was 35 then, Joe was 55, which seemed old to me at the time, but Joe was a great guy to run with. He wouldn't hesitate to stop for a drink or take in a Honky Tonk, if we had the time to do it. He did object to me eating Mexican food and then climbing into the sleeper. He said he had to drive down the road with his head out the window when I did.

I was in excellent shape in those days and Joe wasn't in too bad of shape, but looking back, I should have been more careful about a situation that happened on one particular trip. We headed over the mountains to Selah to load up Tree Top Apple Juice for Safeway warehouse in Santa Fe Springs, California. When we backed into the dock the fork lift driver said they were closing in 30 minutes, there wouldn't be enough time for us to get loaded. Mannnn... we didn't want to lay overnight just to get loaded, so I told the fork lift driver, "we can load this trailer in 30 minutes if you can keep up. "He laughed like hell, not believing me, and then... he gave in and said, "You better keep up because I'm going to be hauling ass with these pallets." I asked Joe if he was up to it and he was real game, so I told the forklift driver to get on his bicycle and start pedaling! I put Joe to my right, got into overdrive, and away we went! The cases were nice and square and that's good, but they did weigh 64 pounds and it's a real good work out. I looked out the corner of my eye and Joe was putting out every ounce of energy in his body. By the time we were half way through the trailer, the fork lift driver was slowly dropping behind, and Joe and I were smoking him! We didn't throw up that last case too soon because Joe was maxed out, and when I look back in time, he very easily could have had a heart attack, but he didn't. The fork lift guy was happy, he said he really didn't think we could do it, but we did. When Joe recovered, he was like a young kid bragging to anyone that would listen, of the Great feat we had accomplished. It made me feel good too, especially for Joe, but I had done stuff like that before. That night as I was driving over the Syskous in the snow, I felt pretty good about things, and so did Joe as he was sacked out in the sleeper.

    I had been running with Joe Hester for about 2 months when Jim Jamerson contacted him. He was looking for a driver to take over a rig that he had put on with ONC Alfreight. Jim was the Line driver at ONC, that drove the Tri-Cities run 6 years back in in 1967 when I was loading his trailers every night. He was still a driver there full time while putting this rig on with the over the road division of ONC. He had worked with Joe at LASME years before and they knew each other real well. Jim said he had a cowboy relative that was driving his rig now, but wanted him off as soon as possible, and wanted a good, reliable driver to take it over. Joe highly recommended me!

    Before I leave Joe, and go to work driving Jim's unit, roll & rest, I have to tell the story of one adventure Joe & I had with Mexico. We were told to go to Nogales and pick up a full load of boxed shrimp. When we got to the Mexican border, this was a whole new experience. NAFTA was about 25 years into the future yet and the way we picked up the load was by transloading. Here is how that worked. We would back our trailer up to the border. The Mexican would back his trailer up to ours. We would bucket brigade the freight until there was a little distance between and then set up the gravity rollers. Joe & I in our trailer and the Mexicans in their trailer. Between Joe & I, I know we got an exact count on every case of shrimp. I had done stuff like this so many times. When our trailer was fully loaded and Joe signed off on the bill of lading, or a reasonable facsimile thereof, I know we had a perfect count. When it came time for the delivery to the customer, somehow, and someway, Joe's load was 3 cases short. To this day, I do not know how that was able to happen, but it did. I don't know if Joe had to finally pick up the tab for that shortage, but I know they were trying like hell to stiff him in the beginning. That shrimp per case was very expensive even back in 1973.

Jim had one of the new GMC Astro tractors with a 318 Detroit engine and those huge glass wind shields. His offer was a little strange because he referred to me as a silent partner. I was given the going rate, which was a percentage, and then he would add 1% of the overall profit. Anyway you would look at it, it wasn't a job I was going to get rich off of, but I had a whole lot of independence. It was also an approved Union job.

I wasn't on that rig but about 2 months and Jim bought another tractor. It was a Deluxe Mack Cab Over, and it had only 70,000 miles on it. It had a real nice 350 Cummins engine; RT-00-913 transmission, do 95 mph in the 13th hole. A logging outfit down by Mossy Rock bought this unit with the idea of running it on the road. It had a nice Utility refer trailer to go with it. After 30 days on the road, he bagged the road work, parked the trailer and put the tractor to hauling logs, then put the tractor & trailer up for sale. Jim bought the tractor & trailer, got it permitted with ONC Alfreight and turned it over to me. I really liked the entire unit. The hockey puck suspension gave it a hard ride at times but it had a 240 inch wheel base and I could keep it stretched out all the time except for certain scale houses. Things would go pretty damn good for a while! Jim hired another driver, Miles Hall, to drive the Astro I had gotten off of, and as things would shake up down the road, he and I would have an encounter that I will talk about later.

So… things get pretty routine for the most part. I would run to LA a lot, and then run between LA & Phoenix for 10 days to 2 weeks. Catch a load home and unwind for about 3 days and do it again. Joe Hester had since gotten off his rig and hired Fred Conolly to run it for him. I already knew Fred and he and I got along great! We liked to get loads to the same area running south, and run together. One particular week, we had loaded on a Friday afternoon, with loads both going south of the Bay Area. He had one for Burlingame, I had one for Fresno. We could take off on Saturday afternoon, run just south of Eugene and lay in the rest area that night. Take off on Sunday morning and run into our destination, giving us time to be first in line to unload on Monday morning.

The Cool Apple Express

Sunday morning, we take off from the rest area south of Eugene and head down the road. It's a nice, comfortable Sunday morning, real laid back. As I am unconsciously looking out my side window, I sense an uncomfortable feeling, the car running next to me is trying to stay at my pace and I take a wide eyed look. Unbelievable!! Here's a guy in his birthday suit, driving his car south on I-5 on a beautiful Sunday morning, wacking his Johnson. If you are a real man, it gives you an awkward feeling to observe something like this. If you speed up, so does he, if you slow down, so does he. Once it all sets in, it really becomes comical. I didn't know at the time that he had been doing this to Fred, who was running about 1/3 of a mile behind me, before he started doing it to me. What did this guy do, walk out his front door, get into his car naked and just start driving? I didn't see clothes anywhere in the car. Finally, the guy disappeared. I pulled over on the top of Rice Hill where we always bumped our tires. Fred pulled in up ahead of me. Fred climbed out of the cab and he's laughing so hard he can't stand up. It's so contagious, I start laughing, neither one of us can hardly talk. We were laughing so hard we were crying. Once we got back on the road again, it was pretty quiet for a while. About 30 minutes from Medford the "naked master baiter" appears again. He had to be running over 200 miles in that condition. When we finally pulled into the truck stop in Medford we were back to laughing like hell again. The waitress wanted to know what was so funny, so we told her!

The runs between LA & Phoenix paid the same as a full run up to Seattle, so, it was beneficial to get those Phoenix runs, only 400 miles vs. 1100. You wanted to try and make those Phoenix runs at night. The desert is just too hard on the tires during the daytime. Even though it's still 100 degrees at night, you don't have the sun beating down on the asphalt which can disintegrate a tire. One night I was running with another rig, and I'm guessing we were loaded about the same for weight. I knew we were geared different because, he could inch ahead of me in some spots and I could inch ahead of him in others. The desert can be deceiving, there are a lot of pulls out there even though the terrain doesn't look like it. My tractor, being designed by a logging company, had put that OO-913 transmission in it, and in the top hole, it would do 95 MPH. I ran for many miles with that other rig, and we were back and forth like I said, but then… I pulled ahead of him in this one spot, and I figured I would open his eyes. I worked it to a spot where I could get enough rpm's to make an upshift, and I did, and shifted it into the 13th hole. I pulled away from him, he was topped out at his top speed and rpm's. I was up at 85 mph and kept it there for awhile, put some distance between him & me and then eased back to a sensible speed in the 12th hole. I only did that 2 times the whole time I was driving that Mack, and it was probably 2 too many.

There was this nice little bar in Montebello, and even though we usually didn't spend any more time in our yard there than we had to, we did patronize the bar there once in a while. We usually were only in the Montebello yard (LA) to conduct business, or, if it was at night and we would crash in our sleeper. One particular night, Fred & I are staying in Montebello waiting for the next day to get a load. Instead of sleeping in our respective sleepers (Cab), we decided to get a motel room close to the bar, get cleaned up and party a little. The bar was always full of working girls, and a good opportunity to have a little fun if you had the time. They had a little dance floor, a small band, and it was real easy to meet someone there. I wasn't in there very long and I was sitting and talking with this one solo lady. She told me she owned a motel just down the road and invited me to come down. She had a car, I jumped in and away we went to her place, the motel. At first, everything seemed real normal to me. Things were going by the numbers. When we got to the motel and got out of her car, I followed her and, I noticed as we were moving down hallways and going through doors, she was locking all the doors behind us. When we got to the place where she actually resided it was like being in someone's house. But Wait! There's More! The next few minutes for me were like out of a horror movie. We are in this woman's bedroom and everything goes into a Jeckel & Hyde scene for her. She pulls off her wig and her whole personality changes, and the entire picture is changing before my eyes. I'm thinking, I WANT OUTTA HERE! I go out the last door I came in and I'm going down this hallway checking all the doors and they are all locked. It was like being in a maize, and I will admit, I didn't panic, but I had some real eerie feelings. I finally worked my way to where I was at least outside, but there was no doors or pathways to the outside world. I was in this, like, open atria, it had big concrete blocks on all 3 sides, a wall about 10 feet high, with the 4th side being the motel structure. I kept leaping up until I could get my fingertips over the edge of the concrete blocks, and I pulled like hell till I could get high enough and get a leg on top and over the blocks. I pulled myself completely up, and then, dropped to the ground on the other side. I'M OUT! It was little over a mile up the hill to the bar, and I jogged the whole way in loafers and slacks. I walked into the food section of the bar & restaurant and there was Fred, eating. He was real surprised to see me. He thought I was taken care of for the night. I told him how happy, and glad I was to get into a normal situation again. Real glad that crummy experience was behind me! Sometimes you never know what lurks behind the next corner.

Miles Hall came to work at ONC Alfreight on Jim Jamerson's Astro, almost immediately after I had gotten off of it and I started driving the Mack. I never really got to know him, matter of fact, he was no more familiar to me than some stranger off the street. I had exchanged a few words with him in the driver's room in Montebello a couple times and they were very brief exchanges. Since we both drove rigs for the same person it would only seem natural that we would probably have something in common, but it just didn't happen. I had no feelings about the man one way or another, I didn't know him. I had driven the Astro for about 2 months, and now I had been on the Mack driving about another 4 months, and I felt Jim was real happy with the way I was handling his equipment and doing the trucking. Counting the 2 months I had run sleeper with Joe Hester, it totaled about 8 months driving for Alfreight. Miles was a good sized guy, bigger than me. We were about exactly the same age. One afternoon, he and I were both sitting in the driver's room in Montebello making some small talk for really the first time. Nothing violent, threatening, or, out of the ordinary. All of a sudden out of the blue, he starts demeaning me and telling me to mind my own business. His voice had a very challenging tone as if to say, "Shut the fuck up or I'll kick your ass." I had one of my natural responses, I told him, "if you feel that bad about it, maybe you and I ought to step outside and discuss it." "I'll step outside with you anytime big man." he says. I was the first one out the door into the lot. It was a bright sunny day, no eye hazzards what so ever. He was right in front of me and I gave him a straight shot to the face, and he quit immediately. I don't know what was the biggest shock, him giving up so easily, being the big man he was, or, the fact I had broken my hand. The fight was over with that one blow, and so was the fight for my job. When I had gotten back to Seattle, the Montebello office had already called Jim Jamerson and told him they expected him to fire me, that I wasn't allowed back in their yard anymore. On top of that, I had this crazy load of candy going into Portland, 2400 boxes of every different size. It was tough driving the 1100 miles with a broken hand. I hired 2 lumpers in Portland to unload the trailer for me. When I got back and found out I didn't have a job anymore, that was kind of a letdown. I had to suck it up one more time and move on, which I did.

After a brief period of time, partying, resting and putting myself into a different frame of mind, I started making trips for Joe to Chicago. I would actually stick it out for almost 3 months before I got off the truck this time. I was working the Hall in early December 1973. It was in late November that I found my dog Vantage, as a pup, near Vantage doing a Vantage turn for BestWay. Brought her home and had the great relationship I had with her for 13 years. Will the Gypsy ever settle down for good? That thought would roll around in my brain a lot.

1974

ANOTHER MIXED BAG

I HAD BEEN SITTING around a little after the 1973 Holidays. The weather was crummy and there was a lot of football to watch. The phone rings and Dascher is on the other end of the line. He had a trip for me to make to Portland if I could go. He had some deal worked out with a cabinet maker and would haul these cabinets from time to time, I had hauled them to Boise, Idaho one time. Typical nasty Northwest winter weather. Alternating between wet snow and cold as hell rain with a pretty swift breeze, just what you would expect. The tractor was a conventional Pete with a 335 Cummins and no Jake brake. Had a 13 speed and was a pretty decent piece of equipment. Little did I know at the time this trip was going to turn out to be a marathon. Jack initially told me one trip to Portland. I assumed he had a back load. I ran down to Portland with the load, got it unloaded and gave a call back to find out what I was hauling back. They sent me to this yard to pick up a full load of rebar headed for Idaho Falls, Idaho. I left the side boards on the trailer except for the rear. Chained everything down good. I know it's 700 miles from Seattle to Pocatello, don't know exactly how far it is from Portland to Idaho Falls, but it has to be somewhere around that distance. I took off on I-84 heading east, it was getting colder and the rain & snow mix was all snow now. Not snowing real hard but, I know what it's like in the Blue Mountains, and if we got this now, it most likely will be heads up in the Blue's.

Somewhere four hours east of Portland on I-84, in the night, I pulled off the road and faded into the sleeper. After getting up and getting going again, it wasn't long till I was running in the Blue Mountains and with this nice heavy, solid load of rebar, I had a great load to be running in winter conditions and it might just keep me from chaining up. It was snowing but not real hard. The road was compact snow & ice. I ran I-84 all the way to Mountain Home, Idaho where I went east on state Hwy. 20. It was dark again. There was hardly any traffic out on 20, but… the highway was glare ice all the way, and you would be able to see your face if you were standing and looking at the road.

I was getting near Idaho Falls and started monitoring the CB, I wanted directions to a good truck stop. It was about 8 at night and I was so damn hungry. All the locals that were on the radio would bend over backwards to help you. They guided me right into the "Big Bear" truck stop and there was lots of room to park in the back. I went in and ate big time. No place to shower but I was sleeping alone, so who cares. I checked this big thermometer in the window and if I remember right, it said something like 20 degrees outside. I shut the engine down and climbed into the sleeper. Slept like a rock, and when I woke up it was clear skies and sunshine but cold as hell in the cab. I started the engine, put on some clothes and went into the truck stop to relieve myself. When I looked at the thermometer again it said 6 below zero. If I had known that it was going to drop that low, I would have let the engine idle all night, but it started up, so, everything was OK.

After having a hearty breakfast I was going to see if there was any chance of getting this load off on a Saturday. I called the number I had for the customer and I'll be darned, he said he would meet me and unload the rebar. We met up at the designated location and everything went well. He signed off for the product, I used his phone to call back with Dascher to see what he had for me. His answer? "Find a broker and get a load somewhere!" Ha, Ha, Ha, Ha. Idaho Falls was not a big place in 1974, and as far as a shipping hub, I didn't know what to expect, especially on a Saturday.

    I looked in the local phone book and found a broker that was open. He asked me if I was equipped to haul a full load of grain to Vallejo, California. I explained to him what I had as a trailer and side boards and he said, "You can do it!" I got the directions and headed for American Falls, which was about 60 miles south. When I got down there, I did have to find a way to jerry rig the rear board to make sure it would hold, and not leak. Got two chains criss-crossed on the back with binders as tight as I could get them. They loaded me up at the silo, I tarped the load and I was set to travel for Vallejo. It was getting late in the afternoon, but I was all loaded up for my next stop and it was a pretty long ways away. I was going south on state Hwy 93 expecting to intersect with I-80 at the border town of Jackpot, Nevada. When I got near Jackpot they were saying on the radio that the roads had been shut down because of ice & snow. Aha... that's why I hadn't seen anyone for miles! It was late Saturday night when I got into Jackpot. I hadn't taken a shower since Thursday morning. I must have stunk to high heaven! I had a girlfriend in Billings, Montana that I would see once in a while when driving for Joe. I knew she left Billings and was living with a pit boss and working in Jackpot. I even knew the name of the club she was at. There was a time when she really liked me.

    Because the roads were closed, and even if it was Saturday night, the streets of Jackpot were really pretty quiet. I was actually able to park my rig pretty close the to the club where my old girlfriend was supposed to be working. I got out of the cab and was going to go into the club. So help me God, I looked in the window and there she was big as life. I took one look at myself and said, "Man... you look so bad, and smell so bad, do not go in there and try to make nice." No guts on my part! I chickened out and went back into the cab and crashed! I was so rum dum and tired, I would have looked like a complete dope anyway.

Got up on Sunday morning and drove to Wells, Nevada where I could fuel, shower and eat. That is actually where Hwy. 93 intersected with I-80. It was going to be 400 miles to Reno. Never forgot sitting in that truck stop at Wells eating breakfast. They had these brand new shirts and coats hanging in view that you could purchase. The most beautiful boxed-back coat I have ever seen was hanging there. I wanted that coat so damn bad! I had to hang onto my money because, I didn't know when this marathon was going to end. They wanted $60 for that coat in 1974. I didn't wind up buying it but, I thought about that coat for a long time after that. So… I headed west for a long boring ride to Reno.

When I got to Reno it was night again, and I had checked my equipment along the way. I noticed an oil seal on one of my bogies was leaking pretty bad. Up to this point, I had been real lucky as far as any mechanical problems, which had amounted to zero. I had pushed things pretty good so, I figured I would find a truck shop in Reno, park in their yard for the night and I would be first in line on Monday morning to get that wheel repaired. Didn't want to go down Donner Pass and have something stupid happen. When they opened in the morning I was able to get permission from up home to get the seal replaced and the shop said it would be ready to go in 24 hours.

I had a pretty good friend from High school named Bob "Reno" Lyons that lived in Reno. I gave him a call and he came down and picked me up. He took me to his place that was only about 6 blocks from downtown. He would normally be working on a week day in some elevator shaft somewhere but, he was temporarily laid off so, we were able to have a nice get together over the next 24 hours. Lots to talk about. Hadn't seen him since I came back from overseas in 1959, and was headed from my leave in Seattle to my next duty station in San Antonio, Texas. I had never met his wife before and she was real nice to me. On Tuesday morning they took me down to the shop and my rig was ready. It was real nice to see you guys!

Down Donner Pass and into California and the Bay Area. I was clean and pretty rested for a change. Getting unloaded was about as easy as falling out of bed. They run you up on this scale/ elevator

The Cool Apple Express

contraption. I pull off the rear board. Get into the cab and they do the rest. Run you up in the air and all the grain flows out the back of the trailer. Now I had to find a load home. Found a broker in the phone book again and he had a full load of tar paper at Owens CORNING Inc. going to Bellevue, Washington. A palletized load of roofing materials, and not only that, it is going to be delivered within 10 miles of the yard. I don't remember the exact town the Owens CORNING warehouse was located but it was in the Bay Area somewhere. When I got there it was raining like hell and it would rain the whole way home. I got into Bellevue Wednesday afternoon right on a construction site. It was out in a bunch of mud and it was still raining like hell. Left on a Thursday morning got back on a Wednesday, late. All the tickets were signed and it wasn't my responsibility to collect the money. All equipment in great shape with no incidents. Dascher didn't say a thing about anymore driving, guess he just wanted to get those cabinets delivered. I was ready for a little free time anyway.

Over the next few days, I still had the taste of Reno Nevada in my mouth and thought I would drive down there and enjoy the place as a footloose civilian for a change. Once I collected my money from Dascher, I got my beautiful 50 Merc ready for the 600 mile trip down to Reno. I made sure I had a few provisions, besides clothes, to sustain me for a while when I got there. The ride down was fine and I imposed on "Reno" to stay at his place temporarily. The next day after I got there I went into the local Teamster hall in Reno just nosing around. I wanted to scope things out and find out what things were like there in the trucking business. I had no idea what was about to take place over the ten minutes I was there.

As I was wandering around in the room at the Teamster hall, I casually, and informally introduced myself to this man that was in there. When he found out I was a driver, he asked me how much driving experience I had. I explained to him what I had done and showed him my Teamsters ID. He then said to me," could you take a driving job now?" I was momentarily stunned, but said, "yes, when would you want me go to work?" He told me he needed a driver right now to drive a tanker load of hot oil to Golconda, Nevada. I was told to drive up to the 76 Truck Stop in Sparks, the tankers were staged there and report in for a load. The company was Telfer Tank Lines out of Martinez, California. They had a high way paving job just east of Winnemucca, Nevada. The tanker was loaded with hot oil and they didn't waste any time getting me on board that unit and headed east. It's about 160 miles to Winnemucca, and another 15 miles to Golconda. There was a lineup of tankers when I got there and then I would pull into this area where they would pump me off. The man on the job there did all the work with the pumping off, you just bided your time talking till it was time to get out of there and head back to Sparks. For tracking purposes, the distance between Reno and Sparks is the width of railroad tracks. That's the only way you would know they are two different towns.

I got the impression after the first trip was completed they were going to use me on a regular basis. I found out there were two drivers to a unit, and two shifts. One driver at night and one driver on day shift. The drivers would switch every week. The driver on 2nd shift would leave the 76 Truck Stop in the evening, go down Donner Pass to Martinez, California, load the hot oil, and bring the load back up to Sparks for the day driver. The day driver had to be a little flexible and try to time when the load had arrived at the Truck Stop. He would check the fuel and all the equipment and then head east to the construction site. I stayed on that job 7 weeks till it was completed. I had come into Reno to goof off, and now, I'm driving every day, or night, for a tanker outfit.

A lot of things happened in that 7 weeks. I met a nice woman there and she became my girlfriend for a while. Wish I would have met her under more stable circumstances. I got pneumonia and was treated at the Veterans Hospital. I laid in the sack for 3 days and then, I was right back driving. I could have croaked, but I didn't, and I worked my way through it. I had rented a shack, and I mean a shack to live in from this crazy woman. I would see her out working in her yard all the time. She had miles of hose weaved through her yard. I was pretty busy, just staying there when I slept, so I didn't get a chance to hang out with her. The driver that drove opposite me on the tanker, his name was Ed Corwin, Ed and I became good friends.

Since I found out the job would be over in 7 weeks, I nosed around to see if there would be anything else in the way of work to stick around for. I did get some half assed promises but, it didn't materialize. So, when they told me this would be the last week of work, I made my arrangements to head back home. I told the goofy lady that owned the shack I was renting I would be leaving and she owed me a cleaning deposit. She knew she owed me the money! When I got ready to leave, she conveniently decided to make herself scarce. OK, I'll find something of value. I rolled up about 300 feet of her garden hose and put it into the back seat of my Merc. It would wind up at my Mothers place and be used for years. I was loaded up and trucking, headed back home!

While I was in Reno I fell in love with this restaurant there called "Louies Basque Restaurant", just across the railroad tracks in Sparks. It wasn't a fancy place, it was kind of rustic. I had never eaten Basque food before, that I remember. The Tables were picnic style and usually only about 5 things on the menu per day. My favorite was, "chicken basque". It was out of sight delicious. To this day, it is my favorite dish. When I got back to Seattle I asked my Mother about that dish. I told her that I remember her cooking chicken when I was real young and it tasted like the chicken basque I had eaten in Reno. Come to find out, she said she had learned how to cook it that way from her Mother. Her Mother was the daughter of an Irish immigrant Mother and a French Basque father. Would have never found that out if I hadn't eaten Basque food. It's still my favorite.

It was a beautiful early spring day when I left Reno, great to be alive. I'll never forget what happened then. I was about 50 miles north of Reno and headed for the mountains, all of a sudden I see this huge rattle snake making his way across the highway. That snake was huge!! He was moving not dead! I could feel him when the car ran over him. It was absolutely stunning! I had never seen a snake that large in my life.

Michael J. Hicks

Mike & the "Toy Sheriff" of Shaniko, Oregon 1974.
One of my favorite pictures.

I made a point of driving up Hwy 97, once I got into Oregon. I wanted to stop in the rural town of Shaniko and have my picture taken with the toy sheriff. He was a jewel and I had the time to do it this trip, and I wanted to get it done for sure. When I was running sleeper with Joe Hester we use to stop in this little café in Shaniko and sometimes we would see this toy sheriff. He had to be in his 80's, he wore this box-backed dress coat and had the hog leg on his side, and the star pinned to the coat. It just cracked me up! So, it's a real sunny day when I get into Shaniko, and it's quiet. I parked the Merc, and asked around for the sheriff. It wasn't hard to find him so, I had somebody take my camera and shoot some pictures of him and me together by my 50 Merc. They are priceless to me! Some of the best things in life are free!

Back in Seattle it's finally spring again and the prospects for a new year are a little brighter now that the dark and gloomy days of winter are over. I did a little casual tanker work, and then, I got a call from Packard & Moss (P&M Transport), a small outfit in

Woodinville. It was run by two good guys, Bill Packard and Mick Moss. I didn't know either of them. Mick Moss did most of the talking and asked me if I could come to Moses Lake for one or two weeks to do a volume tender between Moses Lake and Vancouver/Portland. I said yes, assuming everything was kosher.

Moss was from Alabama and had this charming gift of gab that could lure to do just about anything if you let him. I drove over to Moses Lake, and he critiqued me on what was expected of me. He had rented me a room in this cheap motel, not knowing I would be getting very little sack time there. I would be putting in about 16 hours a day driving, and it only left about 5 hours for sack time when you include any other things that have to be done. It was a 600 mile turn every day, and then there was load and unload time. Sometimes, unloading in Vancouver was real slow. If you didn't get a chance to put food and water in the cab with you, the only time you got a chance to eat, was late, after you loaded the tanks and fueled the truck.

The trip: In order to make the trip interesting and exciting, P&M would not buy a permit to drive on the Oregon side of the Columbia River (I-84). We had to drive on the Washington side, state Hwy 14, 2 lanes. It wasn't too bad till you got down to White Salmon, and then, the interesting spots in the road appeared. First, was the tunnel. It wasn't very long, but really narrow. It would be outlawed to run a tanker in that tunnel if it were in Canada. Every time I got close to the tunnel, I would wonder what I was going to meet in there. If you were to meet another tanker, or semi, it would be a close and hairy experience.

Farther on down the road, you get to "Bridge of the Gods". That is about 20 miles before your destination. That particular spot has to be defined. First of all it's on a curve. Then, even though it's a 2 lane road, I would say at that point, it's really only about a lane and 7/8ths. The west bound lane hugs the cliff, the east bound lane has no shoulder, or guard rail, and it's easily 600 feet down to the Columbia River. You have to slow to a minimum of 25mph, and hope you don't meet any traffic coming the other way. I have!

Coming back empty, in the outside lane, there ain't enough money in the world to get me to look over my right shoulder down on the Columbia. No way!

I've also run I-84, many times, looked up at that point, knowing what's up there, and did a lot of thinking. Every time I had made runs on the Oregon side, I would look up at that particular spot, and be glad I wasn't running up there. That was 36 years ago, and maybe, that has been gone over again and made into a better road.

I finished up that job, and Moss said he would be getting in touch with me real soon, so stand by, and I did. Well, in the beginning, I was pretty flexible and tried to be patient. Moss would always say, "Mike, I'm gonna have lots of work for you. Please hang in there with me. We will call you." For a while, that's the way things would go, it was a feast or famine job.

One stint, I worked 48 straight hours. I was glad to go home. Then, I wouldn't hear from Moss for days. I might take a one day job from another outfit hoping I would hear from Moss. I tried to do it their way, and for about 3 months I did, but I had to have something more absolute than that. I liked Packard & Moss, and we didn't have any personal problems, but I bailed to get something steadier. If P & M had kept me working I probably would have stuck around. They were nice guys to know, I liked their trucks, they kept them up. They hired me in a pinch and that's probably the way they planned on treating me. It was in the prime time of the year and I couldn't waste it on promises that weren't materializing.

I needed to get to work and making a living. I jumped on a truck for Joe, and started making Chicago trips for a while. It became September and I went to WONDER Bread for a student trip and lots of terrible hours.

1975

WONDER BREAD

In September 1974, I got a call from WONDER Bread. They wanted a full time transport driver. I went as directed to take the normal student trip. I had just climbed out of one of Joe Penberthy's Peterbilt's, getting in from Chicago. I met up with Mr. Terry Glover, the truck boss, and he pointed me to the Freightliner we would be going for the driver test in. I checked it out, climbed in, and the both of us were down the highway while he was checking out my driving skills. He showed pleasure in my driving and I was pretty sure when we returned to the plant he was going to hire me, and he did.

The work there was fine. At that moment of being hired, I was thrilled to think I would be getting a good Teamster job where I would be home every day and have a steady pay check every week. There was no down time once you punched in, the work was continuous, and you were busy till it was time to punch out and go home. The equipment was good for a local job and I had no problems with the physical requirements of the job. In all the years I had been in the trucking business, up to this point, the working hours of this job were by far the worse I ever had. That included every crummy job I had, fulltime, part-time, anything, and I'm not talking about putting in long hours, I'm talking about the structure of your entire week. I would go to work around 5:30 PM and work around 'til 4, or 4:30 AM. I worked Sunday & Monday night, had Tuesday night off, worked Wednesday, Thursday, and Friday night, and had sat night off. Because of the way these hours shook out, it was like I never had any time off. It all ran together. Your body is constantly adjusting to changes. I could never get anything done away from the job. I would basically sleep most of my day off and get ready to go back to work again.

This is a good time to bring up a little episode that took place so unconsciously, and might even be a little amusing. With the terrible hours I was working it was paramount for me to try and get some adequate sleep. I was sharing a condo over in Kirkland with a good friend of mine and I had the Master bedroom, it was almost like having your own apartment. Ed, the buddy of mine I shared the condo with, he worked days, so, with my crummy hours, I didn't see him all that much, and then, he moved into a cheaper place to save money. I would get to bed about the time all the people in the condo would be either showering to go to work or revving their cars in the garage below to get out of the building, and then came the construction. I would get so pissed off trying to sleep, sometimes I would jump in my car, drive across the lake to Moms house and try to crash in the back room there. On one of these occasions I had done just that. I was in the back bedroom at my mother's house and had just got to sleep. My Mother was gone and I was pretty sure I could log some Z's for a while. The doorbell rings. I'm in my birthday suit and I don't care who it is. I get up, walk into the living room and open up the door. Standing on the porch is a lady from "Watch Tower" and I'm standing in front of her looking her straight in the eyes. I didn't have to say a word. I'm sure it cured her from ever stopping at mom's again.

I did this for 6 months, kept perfect attendance, and the day after I quit, I was actually looking forward to getting on one of

The Cool Apple Express

Joe's rigs and heading for Chicago. I didn't hate anyone there when I left, I just wanted to get my friggin mind back, that's the truth. It was one huge relief to get back into a normal world, and just feel normal again. The job at WONDER Bread had become like a prison of my mind & body. The change to driving for Joe felt like a vacation. I was a prisoner walking out the gate into one of Joe's Peterbilts. I was giddy! Nuff said about that.

So, I'm running for Joe again, and Joe and I both know it's gonna be short lived. I made about 5 trips, then I got off the truck, signed up at the Teamsters Hiring Hall and got into a nice little groove for a while. The Hall would keep me busy enough, and I was picking up some deals on cars, fixing them up, and making a little money there too. It was a real generic time, nothing to write home about, and I was catching up on my love life that had suffered during my 6 months in purgatory. I did get a little gig during that period of time driving belly dump over on the Eastside that was also semi steady. Still enjoying the relief of shaking off the job at WONDER bread.

One thing I have learned time and time again, at least for me in my lifetime, you never know what's just around the corner, and it happens time and time again. I guess, as a fairly dull period, I guess it was bound to happen again.

It was a normal night and I had stopped off at Jim's Steak House in Lake City. It was a regular stop for me back then, and Jim's was a pretty mellow place most of the time. It had steady people going into the lounge in those days, and I knew most of the regulars. We didn't have much trouble in there as bars go. You might have a little scrape in there once in awhile and that can happen in the best bar in town. So... on this particular un-exciting evening, I'm at the bar having a drink and doing what I would normally be doing. This young guy, about 25, sitting next to me, was running his elbow into me on a pretty regular basis. I told him, "don't you think that elbow is out of control?" He spun around and started throwing punches at me and the fight was on. The fight flowed into the little dance floor where the one man band was playing full tilt. I didn't realize that about 4 of these guys had come into the bar together, and when the fight started, I was fighting more than one guy. I was just throwing punches and more than two arms were coming my way. The fight poured out into the street (Lake City Way) and I was going after who was ever in front of me. I was in good shape and I didn't worry much about running out of gas, but every fight is different, and it's a survival thing that keeps you fighting on to win out and stay on top.

When we had gotten into the street, I didn't know the one-man-band guy had entered into the fight on my side, and he was a big help. There were 4 of them and 2 of us, and as things were going now, they were going pretty good. It was at about this time, 3 different law enforcement agencies roll up at the exact same time. King County Sheriff; Washington State Patrol; and the Seattle P. D. Guess who was the first person they go after?

I had this guy on the ground after running his face over the right fender of my Pontiac and crushing my radio antenna. I had smacked him a few times and then looked over my right shoulder at the cops coming at me. It was in that instant that Rosie the bartender charged towards the cops and said, "Don't put your hands on him, he's one of the good guys." That saved my bacon! They probably would have sapped me into another Universe. Rosie pointed out the trouble makers and I was on top of one of them.

One of the sad outcomes from this incident was, a guy named Harry, that drank there a lot with his wife, had taken a few shots from one of the punks and was lying on the ground. Harry was in his 50's back then, and a Line driver for ONC. He knew so many of the old drivers from around town that I knew, and I didn't have time to know that he had tried to enter the fight.

Things started to calm down and the excitement was over. A year later they would have a big party at Jim's to celebrate "The Big Fight". It was close to closing time and I headed up to Moms house to clean up. She only lived 2 miles away and when I got to her house, she told me Rosie had called, and told her all about the fight. I cleaned up, and sat and talked to Mom till about 4 AM. I was headed to my bungalow on Dexter Ave., and then… I decided to go down to The Dog House and have me some of their great

The Cool Apple Express

Hot cakes. It was about 6 AM before I headed up Dexter. When I got to my place, I fooled around for a couple hours trying to wind down, 'cause what the hell, I can sleep all day, right? Hit the sack about 8:30 and the phone rings at 10. I was out like a light and almost paralyzed from deep sleep when I answered the phone.

The phone call was from Consolidated Freightways Tank Lines, part of the biggest trucking company in America, and they asked me, "Do you want to go to work for us"? The lady on the other end of the line was holding my resume, and I didn't even remember leaving one there, but I did, and I said, yes. I would like to go to work for you. She told me to bring a few clothes, my shaving kit, and that I would be going to Provo, Utah, after I took the student trip. They wanted me down there now! OK, I jump into the shower, grab my stuff, make fast tracks for East Marginal Way and CF Tank Lines.

When I got there, I got introduced around to the people, and it was a good feel. We were waiting for the Safety Man to get there to give me the student trip. Meanwhile, the other paper work was being taken care of, and the student trip was the only thing holding us up. My driving partners name was Dick Dycus, and it would turn out to be a good set up for both of us, we got along fine. It was late afternoon before the Safety Man got there, and then we started the student. He had me hook up a set of freight doubles. We went all the way to North Bend before we turned around and came back. I saw no problems at all, and the Safety Man says to me, "You got a bad attitude!" Quietly in my mind, I say, where is he going with this? I'm beat tired, had a big fist fight last night, that I didn't start, and this asshole out of the blue says, I have a bad attitude. I looked right at him and asked, what do you mean by that? He told me that my driving skills were fine, but, "there are other important things to driving." He claimed I didn't check the mirror on the passenger side enough to suit him, and that my driving presence was just a little too arrogant!?! That meant I had a bad attitude? I passed the student trip and could make the trip to Provo, but he was going to give me another one in the future. Hmmmmmmmm

Dick and I pull out of the yard about 6 PM, and we are finally on our way. By this time I feel like I have been up for 3 days, and now I have to go to work. It had been a pretty warm day in June and guess what, we can't shut the heater off. The heater is stuck in the On position and will not shut off! We're in western Washington now but wait till we get over the mountains and beyond, this is just the beginning of heat problems. The tractor was OK, it had a 300 Cummins with a 4x3, a little under powered from the Pete's I would drive for Joe, but it was fine, except for the heat.

I think I took the wheel early on so that Dick could get use to me at the wheel, and I could get use to the equipment. Because of the late start, and the fact we both had to get use to each other, I don't think either of us could sleep that first night out, no matter how tired we might be. When I first climbed back into the bunk, it was so hot in there, there was no way I could sleep. It was like a Sauna! The next day we were out in Idaho, the sun beating down and it was hot outside and inside. With the temps into the 90's, Dick and I were having fits about not being able to shut off the heater. It was pretty late in the evening when we arrived at the Cryogenics plant in Provo, Utah. It was 100 degrees outside and our heater was blazing away. It took a few hours to get the Cryogenics loaded and then… we hightailed it for the first truck stop we could find. We got a mechanic to put a T in the heater line and shut that damn thing off. What a relief!! On our way back to Seattle we had stops in Portland, and Centralia down loading the Cryogenics, and the first trip for CF Tanklines was complete, and a success. The next few months would be very busy and the excitement would be over the top.

C F TANKLINES

A GOOD PLACE TO WORK BUT BAD EQUIPMENT—GOOD PEOPLE

My first trip for C F Tanklines, a sleeper run, (sleep??) was finished, and everything came out on a positive note. I had no inkling what to expect, now that I was in the rotation, how I would be used to the Max on my log book. In the meantime, I just wanted to get into the covers of my bed and sleep my ass off. It had been about 5 days since I had any quality sleep, and in a real bed. I was totally wiped!

Sleeper runs were common, but most runs were solo, and in the tanker business, it was normal to max out your daily hours. You were allowed a 70 hour work week in a 7 day period. A 16 hour day was the most you were allowed and there would have to be an 8 hour break with no driving before you could work again. Your log book would be with you at all times while you were on duty and you never knew when a scale house or, a WSP would pull you over.

I got a call real soon and the work began. Runs up to Vancouver B C on a regular basis. The slurry run down to the Centralia steam plant, 2 runs a night, which usually came out to be a 13 hour shift. Back into the prehistoric Liquid Carbonic bulk plant next to Boeing Plant II. You loaded the tank with slurry, run to Centralia and pump it off. They used the slurry to wash the coal that was burned in the steam plant. When you finished the trips, you would stink like slurry, and have one dirty pair of pants. It was a good run, I liked it. I was maxing my hours out every week. I'll have to admit, after a while it can tire you out a little, but that didn't bother me, what bothered me most about working at C F, the rotten equipment you had to drive & operate. I was always pretty handy about fixing the little things, but there was always something wrong with the equipment. It was so time consuming, and having to call for mechanics all the time was a real pain.

The dispatcher was a good guy, and you could joke around and be yourself. One beautiful lady working in the office, that didn't hurt either. So, I'm in the groove working a ton of hours, and not having much time off to get into any trouble. I get a day off and what do I do? Take a busmans holiday. I go to visit my buddy Rock out on his job east of Everett.

Rocky was working on a job down in Lowell, working for the Lowell Brick Co. Lowell is east of Everett on the west side of the Snohomish river. There was a huge clay bank down there that made for natural ingredients in making bricks. Rocky's job was to use this big, older Cat, to paw away at the clay bank, and drag big chunks of clay to fall and roll down. It was definitely a low overhead way, but dangerous way, to get building materials down. It was obviously workable. As I pulled up in an area away from the bank, Rocky spotted me and got off the Cat, and walked over to where I was parked. He pointed out what was happening, and it was plain to see a big chunk of that natural clay could cause real problems, if it got loose and you couldn't get out of the way. As we stood there talking, a big piece of clay fell off the bank, rolled up onto the Cat, and was blocking the stack from breathing. He said, "I better go clean that off and knock down that big chunk still on the bank". I was looking directly at the Cat, with the entire bank in view. Rocky was

The Cool Apple Express

on the front of the Cat, the Cat faced to the bank, his back to the bank, and cleaning off the clay on the hood of the Cat. Cleaning it away from the stack. In an instant, I saw this huge section of clay separate from the bank, it was directly in line with the Cat, and I yelled at the top of my lungs! "ROCKY… DIVE FOR THE CANOPY, THE BANK IS COMING DOWN". I was yelling my lungs out and he dived for the canopy. It was the only protection available. The huge chunk of clay came rolling down and then onto the front of the Cat. This, all happening in an instant, and my heart is really ramped up at this time. Rocky reached the canopy but not unscathed. When the huge chunk of clay rolled up on the front of the Cat, one of Rocky's legs didn't make it completely out of the way, and the chunk rolled over his calf. He was in real pain and I got on the company radio to let them know about the accident. We got Rocky to the hospital in Everett and he had internal damage to his leg. It would wind up keeping him off work for a year and a half. His brother Bob would always say, "I'm glad Mike was there". Rocky would always say, "If Mike hadn't been there, it never would have happened".

It was not unusual for Rock and me to invite some kind of action to come our way in some form or other when we were together. Had to be the combination of the vibes. It wasn't long before this incident happened, that I visited him on another construction job near downtown Seattle. There was an overpass on lower 4th ave. about 12'6", and while he and I were standing and talking, a semi comes through, 13' 6". He was only going about 25 mph, but he hit that overpass with a foot of that trailer, and wacked the shit out of both the trailer and the overpass. The overpass was marked and, you gotta know about those things when you are in the trucking business. There are no excuses! I felt bad for the driver, but it was like going to a demolition derby and we got in for nothing.

The trip I'm about to embark on is one I will never forget. It starts out very run of the mill, like most trips do. This time I get to run along with another driver, and sometimes that makes it nice. We both had pneumatic tankers, empty, and had to dead head almost

350 miles to Valley, which is 60 miles due north of Spokane, on the route to Coleville. The other driver was a brand new hire, and I felt obligated to help out if needed. It was daytime when we started out, and the other driver was having troubles with his equipment, almost from the git-go. Looking back, it probably would have been smart to send the other driver back, but we didn't. We were stopping constantly, just to remedy things and try to keep him going.

When we got to the top of Vantage (Rye Grass), I went over some things on his tractor and we were going again, down the hill (11 miles) and across the Mighty Columbia, up the other side. Made the left turn before Spokane and headed north for the last 60 miles. It was about 10 at night when we got to Valley. The whole little town was built around a big pile of silica sand. It was 1930's state of the art equipment running the plant. They started loading our tanks and, if I had known better, I would have had a hat on that would have covered my entire head, but I didn't. Little did I know, I would be pulling sand outta my scalp for weeks. We're finally loaded, haven't eaten a thing, and we decided to make it to the rest area on I-90, just after we turned right, and we did. The other driver and I were both exhausted, so we both dived into our respective sleepers and crash.

When we both got up early the next morning, the other driver tried starting his tractor and it wouldn't stay running. We finally called C F in Seattle and filled them in on all the hang ups. They told me to get on up to Vancouver B C with my load, that a mechanic was on the way to help the other driver. So, I'm heading for Stevens Pass, and at this point, I figure things are finally going to get routine. I can deliver my load and move on. As I am climbing the east side of Stevens it is starting to rain, and as I come over the top, I see an asphalt crew resurfacing down the west side. I'm watching all this white foam working its way to the surface of the fresh asphalt, because of the rain, and I knew that stuff was going to be just like driving on soap.

No Jake in C F equipment and I have to take care coming off Stevens, but even more so today. I was about one mile from the top going down when I hear the buzzer for the air alarm. I look hard at the gauge and it says 60 pounds PSI, WOW… if it's working correctly it should be around 110 since I'm holding light steady pressure on the brake pedal, I'm in deep trouble! I'm feathering the brakes and keeping the least amount of pressure as I can but, I had to take my foot off the brake, and the gauge would rise slightly. As soon as I tried to feather again, the air pressure would drop again, and the buzzer would come on again. It's six to seven miles to the bottom and I've got a million thoughts going through my mind. I'm trying every trick I think I know, and I'm actually thinking of bailing out. I came real close but… I was still trying to gear down another hole if I could, and then, I got a spot on the downslope that flattened just enough to get it off the side of the road and stopped. One of the guys from the asphalt crew had spotted me from the beginning of my episode, followed me, and as soon as I got it on the side of the road, leaped from his pick-up and sprayed my bogies with his fire extinguisher. In the face of it all, I really only remember certain parts. So much of it was done completely on instincts. I had just had the shit scared clean out of me and, the Good Lord decided it wasn't my time!

We left the rig on the side and the asphalt guy called the WSP for me. The WSP said they would have an officer there directly. The officer arrived, drove me to the first stop at the bottom of Stevens Pass, Alpine Falls. He called C F Tanklines in Seattle for me and they said they would send a mechanic up there. I waited 7 hours and the mechanic finally arrived. One air-line had a hole in it the size of a quarter, and I was back on the road again feeling lucky to be alive.

It's after dark again with a whole day down the tube. By the time I get to Sultan I pull the rig into the huge yard at Bob Hannan's place. I had called his wife Sandy from Alpine Falls, she told me to stop there and I could crash for the night. Bob was doing his thing running the AlCan at the time and I slept like a rock.

Early next morning, I took a needed shower, Sandy fixed me a big breakfast and I continued on to Vancouver B C to unload this sand and finally get home to Seattle. It was a long time before I got the thrill of that trip out of my system. I should have quit after that trip, knowing what the situation was with C F equipment, but I had to get it really pounded into my head.

Enough is Enough! The equip is too much!

So… C F is keeping me real busy, and the battle with terrible equipment just doesn't seem to end for me. It is ruining an otherwise descent job. I had been working at C F for 4 or 5 months by now and was hauling just about everything. This so called genius of a safety man… why isn't he paying attention to all of this bad equipment that won't hold up? Isn't that part of his job too, instead of trying to be some kind of a psychoanalysis? I got a call late in the afternoon to come down and make a trip to Spokane. I had been up all day, so I wasn't rested up. I would be taking a tanker load of cleaning solvent, and it sounded pretty run of the mill. The truck was supposed to have been already checked out by the shop, and released when I came in. Got the tanks filled locally and then headed out I-90 for Spokane. As I was motoring east, just past Issaquah, a set of doubles got along side of me, and the driver was motioning frantically at the rear of my set. I pulled over on the shoulder and, there is a huge flame rising from one of my bogies, cooking the bottom of the tank. I doused the flame with an extinguisher. My knees are a little wobbly at this point. Things are a little cloudy, but I think the driver that warned me, he pulled over too, and called into C F for me.

An hour or two later a mechanic shows up. The story goes like this. The truck had been in the shop for either new brakes, or, maybe it was just a brake adjustment. Whoever did the work had the shoes adjusted to the max on one wheel. They happened to be wedge brakes, and I wouldn't have been able to do anything with them if I could. I adjusted my own brakes all the time but, never wedge brakes. I was real lucky to have that other driver come by when he did. That trailer could have gone off like a bomb somewhere up the road eventually. The fire couldn't be seen from inside the cab.

The Cool Apple Express

I'm about 4 hours into this trip and I'm only 30 miles out of town. The truck was a relic and had a worn out 250 Cummins for power, and boy... I'm just starting to have fun. By the time I get to Denny Creek, mile marker 43, we're starting the climb up Snoqualmie Pass, and I am telling you... I didn't know if this thing was going to have enough gears to get to the top. I could jog faster than we were going. I still have Indian John hill; Elk Heights; the climb to the top of Vantage, and beyond. I'm dead ass tired thinking about it.

When I finally got to Rye Grass (top of Vantage), I pulled into the rest area, and collapsed in the front seat. I slept for an hour and it was tempting to stay there. My fortitude got me going again, and once I got down Vantage, across the Columbia River, and up the other side, I knew it was just a matter of time to get to Spokane, and that was what was keeping me going.

When I finally arrived at the customer, they were waiting for me. One of the brass from C F Spokane was there, and I briefly explained to him why I was late... And I was late! I got to work hooking up the hoses, set the last camel lock, got the power-take-off going and started pumping the solvent. What a display!! All the hoses were like a soaker hose spewing solvent all over hell. I got it shut down and there was solvent everywhere. It was a total embarrassment. Me, and the C F boss, race back to his terminal in his pick-up, and loaded up some good hoses. We raced back to the job site, I hooked up the good hoses and finally got the product pumped off. After loading up all the rotten hoses, taking care of all the loose ends, now I can drive the 300 miles back to Seattle.

I had made up my mind this was my last trip for C F. It was about 11PM in Seattle when I pulled into the yard. Been on the job for 30 hours, No proper rest, no food, nothing but problems with all of the equipment, and on top of that, I'm about 16 hours over legal service hours. I filled out all my paper work, and also wrote a letter to the dispatcher. I wouldn't have been able to work for a few days anyway since my hours were way grossed out. I took way too much pride in my work to have to constantly put up with this kind of stuff. I liked all the people I worked with there but that was enough for me. Within one year of my quitting, C F Tanklines was bought out by Matlack. I was told that, one of the main reasons was, the condition of their equipment. No shit Dick Tracey! You can't be hauling hazardous materials with terrible equipment.

PULLED THE PIN AT C F TANKLINES

I LEFT C F Tanklines in the middle of the night in the fall of 1975. It could have been a fine job but, couldn't get out of the yard hardly without equipment problems. It probably wasn't the best time to leave a steady job but, after 4 or 5 months of close calls with that terrible equipment, I didn't see a future for me there plus, I figured my luck was going to run out on me sooner or later. I had no incidents, or accidents but, I was tempting fate with my luck.

I could always use the Hiring Hall, it had worked good for me in the past. With winter coming on, I knew Joe would be glad to have me make trips to Chicago. I would always have a car I could pick up, fix up and sell. Probably had one going already. The Boeing bust was completely over now, and even though I hadn't found that dream job yet, I seem to be able to keep coming up with enough stuff to keep me plenty busy.

I signed up at the Hiring Hall immediately, and was working a multitude of jobs. You had to realize when you took a job out of the Hall, try to show versatility, and be able to do a lot of different things. The more you could do, the more options you had for work, and a lot of times, one day's work would materialize into several days on a specific job. A lot of times it depended on the impression you made at that particular place of work. I knew a few places they didn't like me the minute I walked through the door. That didn't happen that often but, it did happen. Some places you had to drive rotten equipment and the answer to that was, "I will give you a good days work and you probably won't see me again". For the most part, I always had a positive experience working out of the Hall, and it worked for me.

If Joe knew I was available for work, he would call, and maybe I would go. It was hard to say no sometimes. I could be nice and comfortable watching T V, an hour and a half later, I'm climbing into one of Joe's Pete's and headed for Chicago with a strange sleeper partner. That's the way things went through the winter of 1975 and into 1976.

In February of 1976, I sold my beautiful 1950 Merc. I do not know what possessed me to do that. I regretted that move later on in life but, I did sell it and made fairly good money for the time period. I had fixed up a 64 Pontiac Pontiac Catalina, put a good running engine in it and that would be my main ride for now. I got a wild hair to drive down to Texas and visit. I hadn't been back for 11 years when I had made my permanent departure to return to my home town of Seattle in1965. I loaded up the Pontiac and headed for Texas. I stayed in Texas for one month visiting friends in Austin, Houston, and San Antonio. I even drove truck one day for some gypo in San Antonio. That was a riot! The pay was so low it was laughable. The equipment… well… it didn't have enough power to pull a sick whore out of the sack. One day was plenty Kemo Sabe. After a month in Texas, I headed back home and had a little fun along the way. My friend Alice flew into Reno, Nevada, met me there and we drove back to Seattle. Remember that night in John Day Alice?

Soon as I got into Seattle, Joe had a load waiting for me going to New York City and I climbed aboard. I made 3 trips for Joe and then got off the truck. I immediately talked with a man named Fergus B., that had a nice rig on with MITCHEL BROS. Running flatbed in the western states would be the latest plan. We didn't waste any time getting going. I had to drop down to Portland and go through MITCHELL BROS. tie down school for 3 days. That was a requirement to be able to drive there and, I actually enjoyed going through that little school. It was really informative for me, you learn a lot more than you think you already know and I was glad I went.

As soon as that 3 days were over, I had a load on and was trucking. It wasn't till I had been driving there for 3 weeks that Fergus B got into the details of me being paid. That turned out to be kind of a shocker. He informed me that I would not realistically get paid for a couple of months. The picture of the nice rig I was driving, along with the nice couple that owned it, seemed to change for me at that point. I explained to Mr. Fergus B, that I was never under any impression I would have to wait two or three months for my first check. He kept saying the same thing over and over, and that, I could draw money until then.

No! That's not the way I wanted to do it and, we agreed to disagree. At that point, he told me I wouldn't get any pay for up to 3 months. This is not good! I told him I wanted my money owed me now! He said no. I went to the Washington State Labor Board and filed a complaint against him. I liked the people; I didn't want to have a beef with them; they really didn't give me any choice. It should have never come to this but it did.

I immediately took a one day job from the Hiring Hall, which put me on the water front hauling containers all day. While I was on a coffee break there, I ran into a really neat old veteran trucker I knew from LASME, Mr. Harold Riggs. He was close to retirement and driving local heavy duty. We talked about everything under the sun and I told him about my latest trucking experience, and, that I was looking for a good steady job. Harold gave me an excellent tip, that really paid off. He told me about a new container outfit just starting up in Tacoma, and they were called TOTE. A company called SYSTEM TRANSFER, in Seattle, had just secured a contract to haul their containers. He gave me all the info he knew about it, and I figured I would beat a trail down there directly as soon as I could.

System Transfer

I went down to System the day after talking to Harold. It was just across the street from the old truck stop on 6th ave. For some reason, I had barely heard of this outfit. Don't know why! I had been up and down 6th. Ave. a million times, but for some reason, System never registered. I went to their loading dock where the dispatch office was located. I didn't know one soul there and this was an alien area for me. The dispatcher was Jim Salvatore, and when I told him why I was there, he acted pretty sour to start out with, but I stuck with it, and he and I got into a pretty heavy discussion about what I knew and what I could do. He asked me where this place was; where that place was, and he went on like this for a while trying to trip me up, like an oral test, and then... I said to him, "Where is Dibble ave. N.W.?" He cracked up and from that moment on, he was a real cool guy to me. Jim and I turned out to be good friends, and I really liked Jim from that moment on. He told me, "come back here tomorrow morning and I will put you to work."

I was there the next morning on the dock, and stood around with my mouth shut waiting for some kind of job assignment. All the drivers were there crowded together, Jim stood up with a list and started calling out names, giving job assignments. At the very end, he called to a driver, Chuck Iten, "Take Mike for a student trip and see if he can drive." We climbed into Chuck's Ford tractor, bobtail, and I headed it down 6th. Ave. We didn't go very far, a couple of miles, and then back to the dock. Chuck yells to Jim, "What you got me checking his driving for, he should be checking mine." The ice was broken and I was given a driving assignment.

At the end of the day, the area outside the dock was packed with guys fueling their equipment. One of the guys that called himself "The Dago", came over to me smiling and started talking. He invited me over to the Transport Grill on Airport Way to down a few beers. I met a lot of the guys and they couldn't be nicer. For awhile, it would get to be a habit of stopping in there, mainly for the social side of things.

The Cool Apple Express

Working at System, especially in the beginning, was an enjoyable place most of the time. It was quite a bit different working there compared to the places I had been for a long time. Most of the guys had just driven locally. There was kind of a different kind of work mentality, it wasn't hard to adjust to but it was different. I just figured I would adapt to their way of doing things and roll with the tide.

I had officially gone to work at System on 11 July 1976, they were real busy. Some nights you would not be done till mid-night if you had a real late TOTE, and you still had to be down at the dock by 7:30 in the morning. Still, it was great for me in the beginning months, I was home every day and the work was steady. It had been awhile since I had been in a desirable position like this. The equipment wasn't all that great, but I wasn't driving all that far either, and they did upgrade the equipment not long after I got there, so it was good.

In a way, for me, working at System was like belonging to a club, and always being involved in a non-stop popularity contest. That's not all bad, it made things kind of fun a lot of the time. Most everybody had a good sense of humor, and everyone was always waiting for someone to drop the next joke. Pretty much a fun loving bunch of guys. Each personality had their own distinctive way, that's for sure.

I was at System for 2 years, with an absence gap in the middle, and it was over some petty stuff that could have been handled in a lot better adult way, but wasn't. The actual trucking that I did was so generic, and unspectacular that, it really isn't worth trying to conger up something exciting to talk about. No wrecks; no blizzards; no coming of mountain passes with no air, it was just pretty routine stuff, work wise. I made a few friends that I am still in touch with today. System was a good company with good guys, and after 2 years I took my hat and moved on. Just an old sweet song keeps Texas on my mind.

Oh yeah! How could I possibly forget GIRL SCOUT COOKIES?? I do have to talk about Girl Scout cookies because…

once a year, usually for one week, System Transfer handled Girl Scout cookies.

The guy that ran System Transfer was very conscious of the company making money. Hauling Girl Scout cookies had to be the one time when he looked the other way, for whatever reason, and made the decision to do that job once a year. There is no way in hell the company could possibly pay union wages and make money hauling Girl Scout cookies.

I remember this one year it was our turn again and here is how my contribution took place. I was teamed up with Barney Miller. Not his real name but everyone had a nick name there, and Barney Miller sounded real close to his real name so he became Barney Miller. No one ever mentioned his real name and I don't even remember it. Barney was a big guy with a real big head, physically of course. Everyone I knew liked Barney Miller. So easy going it would be an impossibility to not be able to get along with him. If everything came to a stop for at least 10 minutes, Barney would be asleep.

So Barney and I are teamed up, and we have two Whoopee trucks full of Girl Scout cookies and headed to north Seattle near about 80th and Roosevelt way. We got to this location and started having troubles from the git-go. We had to get all these cookies inside a building and stored away but for some damn reason I don't remember, we had to feed the boxes through a window from the outside and one guy inside would stack the cookies. Nothing easy. Confirming the old saying,"10 pounds of shit in a 2 pound sack."

Barney and I worked there all day and we were only half done when we were told to finish up for the day. The next day, Barney and I headed back with the rest of our loads to finish the job. That took all day too. Finally... I was thinking to myself, I was so relieved we had the job done and maybe tomorrow I could get a regular job and my sanity back.

I don't think it was the next day, I think it was the following day, when they were passing out work assignments early, on the dock, Jim said, "all those cookies that Barney & Mike delivered have to be picked up from where they delivered them and re-delivered to..." All the air in my sack left my body but, he didn't send me. I think he sent Shirley Temple, (a guy). He did send Barney with someone else though. When I asked Barney later, "did you guys have to take them out the same way we put them in, he said "yes". I really felt sorry for Barney, that job was a turd. Don't know why he didn't send me, I didn't care! Never have eaten Girl Scout cookies since.

Another mixed bag and then... drop the anchor for 4 years

Left System as summer began in 1978. There was a boon of extra jobs and I wound up making some nice trips that paid real good starting with one up to Edmonton, Alberta with a truck trailer load of glass. Soon as I finished that one, I had a stack of 4 new Kenworths to Houston, Texas. Every week for awhile I had a long trip somewhere different.

Rocky's brother Bob... Uncle Bob, known him since the beginning of time. Bob asked me if I would be interested in working for a friend of his named Pete. Pete had a well-known plumbing outfit in north Seattle. He wanted someone to work in a warehouse that was stuffed with equipment, parts, tools, etc., etc., etc. Clean up a lot of stuff, and try to get an orderly mess. I went to the warehouse area and met with, and talked to Pete. We came to an agreement and I started working there the first week of August. August 1978 had to be the wettest in Northwest history. It poured down every day and didn't miss a beat. I was inside the warehouse all day every day, working in the lofts sorting piles and piles of brass fittings. As time went on, I would pick orders, take care of lubing and maintenance on the few whoopee trucks plus on a small single screw tractor that wasn't used that much.

I liked Pete, he seemed like a regular guy. Not much excitement to talk about. Show up at work every day, be a self-starter and try to be as productive as possible. Working for Pete was OK but, Pete knew I didn't belong there, and so... but, before that, I was able to get Pete a nice deal on a Freightliner that was suited real good for the little hauls he had. And then… one day Pete came walking up to me in the yard, and he said, "Mike… I'm sure you need to be working someplace else." It wasn't a hateful type thing, and I knew that, but he felt, and I knew, I was kind of out of place working there, and so, we parted as friends. It was a year later, Pete contacted me and wanted to know if I could find him a good deal on another tractor, and I did. He was pleased as punch. He would get a hold of me again in 1988 and wanted to know if I could find him 2 used flatbed trailers. Did that too, and he couldn't be happier. Matter of fact, I used the 2nd tractor I found for him to go and bring the two trailers to his yard. If I saw Pete on the street today, we would have a good word for one another.

I went right over to the Hiring Hall and looked around, and it wasn't the Hall, but I got word there was work over at Puget Sound Freight Lines. They were located off East Marginal Way and I had seen their trucks forever. I went in there to see about work and bingo, they had me working just about every day. The equipment was descent, you were home every day or night. They had runs everywhere at all hours. I had to show up and take what they gave me and do a good job. I liked working there. Didn't know a soul when I walked through the door. The people treated me fine and I just did my job.

One of my favorite runs was the Triple-Oly. Pick up a full trailer load of glass in Seattle, run down to the Olympia Brewery, spot that trailer, pick up a full trailer load of beer and back to Seattle. Three trips took about 10 ½ hours in 1979. With today's traffic, over 30 years later, who knows what it would be like today. All the time I was at Puget Sound, everything was too sweet, not a good sign for me.

I remember while I was working there, I ran across a real nice guy I would see around occasionally, and that was Louie Engle. I really liked Louie, we had good chemistry, we would talk each other's ears off. Louie wasn't working at Puget Sound but, when he found out that I was doing some driving there, he knew all about the place and we would get into big discussions. Louie was a regular at one of the 2 Teamster Hiring halls and he knew my real close friends Rocky & Bob Hannan. He use to like to bring up their legendary exploits in conversation every time we got together. I remember some years after that, reading about Louie passing away, in the Teamster paper. Louie was the kind of guy that could fit in anywhere, and I felt sad to read his passing.

So... I had been working at Puget Sound Freight Lines as a full time part- timer for about 6 weeks, without a worry in the world and then... I was walking through their yard and this guy stops me. He said he was the Union shop steward and I was now on a 72 hour letter. Since I had never been on a 72 hour letter, I asked him what he was talking about.

We had two Teamster locals in Seattle at that time, that had separate contracts for their work. I guess that is the best way to explain it. Over the years, to this point, I had switched back and forth a few times depending upon the jobs. This 72 hour letter meant, I was expected to transfer from one local back to another before I could turn another wheel at Puget Sound. I made sure I checked in with the dispatch before I left, and that I had been told, and knew what I had to do. So... I walked out to my car and went home. It was Friday and I had the week-end to ponder what to do.

I gave what had happened a lot of thought. I had gotten kind of comfortable at Puget Sound, and it was a jolt to have this happen. What I did next had a lot to do with the way the shop steward handled the whole thing. It didn't sit well even though I knew the Union laws were out there, and I had to abide by them. What I figured I would do is, go into the Hiring Hall on Monday morning, sign up for work and just let things shake out, and that's what I did!

MAKING A DECISION AND 4 YEARS AT LONE STAR

Local 174 still on strike at 8 sand and gravel firms

There has been little or no movement so far in the sand and gravel dispute which has idled about 300 members of Teamsters Local 174 the past three weeks, according to Secretary Bob Cooper.

The strike was called by the members of Local 174 in the pre-mix division after they turned down the final offer by eight of the nine firms in the Seattle King County area. Morale on the picket line has been good; the industry has been shut down. The strike started September 11.

Some 60 members of Local 174 are still on strike against Taylor-Edwards Transfer of Seattle and Kent after the firm refused to be a signator to the negotiated cartage agreement. Picket lines are in force and Local 174 is asking the membership to support these members in any way possible. They have been on the bricks for eight months.

•—LOCAL 174 members Bob Williams, Mike Hicks and Duane Wilcox are aided at their Spokane Street picket line by an unidentified fisherman.

On Strike at Lone Star

Well... I pondered over what to do that weekend, and I figured I would hold tight, go down to the Teamsters hiring hall on Monday morning and just let things play out. It was the beginning of summer and a good opportunity should be out there somewhere. I got to the hall, signed up, and it wasn't long, Ted the dispatcher sent me over to Lone Star on Lake Union. I handed the dispatcher at Lone Star my card and he sent me out to get a dump truck to haul materials all day. Everything went as smooth as possible, kept busy all day hauling out of bunkers to job sites all over town. A big asset for me is, I know every crack in the road in Seattle and that's half the battle. Went to the hall the next morning and got sent to Lone Star again. After a few days of this, Lone Star started calling me at home.

There were 2 dispatchers working at Lone Star, Harvey Richardson., who was the one I got to know and dealt with, and Stan B., didn't have anything to do with him early on, but we would get to know each other pretty well over the next 4 years. Harvey was real nice to me early on, and asked me if I could drive a few other units, I told him yes. He had me drive a truck-trailer rig for the warehouse for a few days, and that worked out fine. I even filled in driving a pneumatic tanker hauling dry cement across town to the batch plant at Spokane Street and Lake Union. All this seemed to be working out great, and then Harvey asked me if I could drive a mixer. I told him I had never driven one, and he had me drive side saddle a couple of days with one of the regulars, and boom, I was assigned to a 7 yarder.

Being at the very bottom of the list, one of the things that happened, you got the oldest piece of equip. to drive. I was used to having better stuff to drive, but you had to take in the value of the whole picture. Here I was being considered to be taken on as full time help if I could maintain 400 work hours, which were the requirement, and really, this was a good Teamster job. I was all for it, especially since I would be working steady, as work permits, home every day, and getting excellent wages and benefits. I worked at connecting the dots and keeping things under control, and it was working out.

The Cool Apple Express

Seattle was in a downtown construction boom at the time, they were building the Seafirst Building, more than one swanky hotel, a new jail, not to mention normal construction jobs around town. I could get called in at 7:30 AM in the morning, and maybe not get away from a job till 9 at night. When they are pouring mud on a job, usually had to go till the job is done. Lots of nights I was out on that job at the jail till 9. If they pulled me off a mixer and sent me to the warehouse to drive semi, that was always a nice touch. Haul pallets of concrete to Tacoma, Everett, Bremerton, etc. The summer of 1979 was a busy one, and I forgot all about Puget Sound Freight Lines.

Things are pretty much getting into a groove, go to work when called, doing what you're told, getting to know the people you are working with. I was driving an old 7 yard mixer, and lots of times get pulled off to haul dump truck, and then, go to the warehouse to drive truck trailer as a fill in, and then, fill in for the guy at night mostly, driving the pneumatic tanker hauling cement across town to the silos at both, Spokane street plant and the Lake Union plant. Backing into the Spokane street plant after dark was a trip. You had to pull up to the curb with the 4-ways on, get out and unlock the gate. Huge rats running between your legs all the time. Once you got the gate open, watch the road closely till there was an open spot, then swing out clear across the entire street and back up as fast as you can. You had to have a picture in your mind's eye of what was behind you because, it would be pitch black and you couldn't see a thing. Once the cab cleared the street, set the brakes, get out, walk back into the yard and scope out how you were going to get back in to unload into the silo. There was conveyors; sometimes mobile compressors in the way you may have to move by hand, there could be all kinds of stuff to clear out. Once you had the path again in your mind's eye, start backing the tanker back in slowly. There was no light, you had to work completely in the dark, so you needed to know where everything was at. I never ran into or over anything but one night… there was a compressor on a trailer right in the way. I had to push it out of the way by hand. I got under it like a blocking sled and pushed like hell. I slipped on the wet and slippery ground and smacked the shit outta my elbow. Got it moved, got the trailer backed in, got the load off and left. Next morning I had to make a trip to the Doc, the bursa sack on my elbow had blown up and the Doc had to drain it. Ah… Well… the price of doing business.

Once I had my feet on the ground, got into the groove, I felt working at Lone Star was a very good Teamster job, not real flashy, but, the equipment was O K, and I had driven the best trucks money could buy, so… this job was starting to mean a lot to me. The group of people I worked with were O K. The older vets were all good, got along good with everyone. The younger crowd had their little cliques and some were pretty good, others were pretty distant, it worked out O K. The lower management/dispatchers. In the beginning, and for a while, that wasn't much of a factor for me. I'm a terrible office clown and I know, unless there is someone I have good chemistry with, someone I feel I can trust, I stay away from the office. Harvey Richardson was basically my main contact at the batch plant, when I went up to the warehouse, Charlie was the guy, and, just do things by the numbers. You know you're going to suck hind tit most of the time, you're new, all you want to do is get along, and do a good job.

I got my 400 hours in, Harvey called me up to the office, he seemed real happy about it, I felt good about it, I was now on the Teamster seniority list, and it meant something. The only problem that would really develop was, the other dispatcher, Stan B, would now start to show me his true colors, and what an evil minded bastard he was. The guy was an excellent dispatcher from the practical point, but, the more time passed, the more I had to deal with him, and see what he did with a lot of other people, not only me, this guy was poison as a person. The work relationship I would have with Stan over the span of time I would be at Lone Star, and that was 4 years, I saw my relationship with him grow worse and never get better. I tried to pin it down several times but the best way to describe it would be, we were running on different tracks and there was no way it would ever change. The strike of 1980 would come along a little over a year after I got there, and that would throw even more gas on the fire with Stan, it would be a situation that would never heal. One of the real funny things about that whole situation was, he fancied himself as a real Romeo, ladies' man and some of the things he would say to the female drivers… if he even pulled a light weight type of that kind of action at Boeing, he would have been drop kicked out of the Human resource office into the middle of Puget Sound. He had about as much tact and diplomacy with women as a dead panther. I think a couple of the women knew the score, they let him run his program but didn't take the bait. He would openly come into the driver's room when one of the women might be there and actually look like he was making a move. They would talk to him with respect, but I never thought for a minute they bought into his action. I think part of it was for the benefit of us male drivers, wanting us to think he was some kind of a Casanova, it wasn't working. So… that was pretty much the way things went the first 15 months I was there, and then we went on strike, and that would turn out to be one adventure for sure.

September 1980 was the beginning of the greater Seattle concrete drivers' strike of which I was a part of. There had been talk since spring of a strike in order to get a new contract and of course it was talked about almost every day. I remember one evening going to a meeting with a lot of drivers not at the Union hall. Only being at Lone Star for about 16 months, and having only one year's seniority, I wasn't all that wild about a strike for a lot of reasons. I personally think it might have been an exciting thing for some, especially the younger crowd to go on a strike and try to show a little power. So… we all went out on strike on a beautiful September day in Seattle Washington. Even though my heart wasn't all that way into it, I was a Teamster in good standing and proceeded to do what I thought was expected of me like I would do with anything else.

September in Washington state is actually my favorite month of the year. In most years, the weather is always great. You have the first Husky home game, and to be up in the northwest corner of the stands, it's about 75 degrees, you got your shirt off and the Huskies are playing on the field in front of you. The Puyallup Fair, one of my all-time favorite places to go, usually starts before the 10th of September. Get to the fairgrounds about 9:30 in the morning, it's a warm sunny day, all the Scones you can eat, the smell of burgers cooking with onions, walk until you've seen it all about 10 times. The silvers (coho) start running in September. You can leave the boat ramp at Shillshole, whip around the point into the bay at Carkeek and catch the evening bite that usually hits between 5 and 6. It will only last for about 15 minutes, but if you are there, you can pick up a couple nice 5 pound silvers and really feel like you've done something. It's usually at the end of September that the switch goes to the off position and you know that summer is over and a lot of serious dark and rainy days are ahead of you.

I was assigned to do picket duty at the Spokane street site and har vee go! We set up shop outside both the east and west gate. All the younger drivers had their new picket signs, they were hoopin and hollering and waving their signs at the traffic going by. I remember there was me, and 3 other guys running football plays near the west gate. I like to be sure of myself in all I do, but I had some uneasy feelings about this whole thing, and, I also knew we had committed, so I had to take command of my feelings about it and do the job that I figured was expected of me and be relied upon if needed, and that is exactly what I did. My friend Bobby Williams (now deceased) was appointed picket captain. Bobby did a good job of taking charge. He had a lot of seniority and it made it easier for him and, he and I worked together a lot during the whole strike.

Very early on, there wasn't too many unusual things happening, and then one day… here come the Mick Santa trucks. They caught us a little off guard, mainly by their initial presence on the scene by roaring thru the gate and I'm sure that was pre-planned. The first picketer standing in their way had to leap to keep from getting run over. Civility would take a hit from that moment on.

The Seattle P D started sending a plain clothes detective to the gates fairly regular and he took a pretty low profile. He was a

The Cool Apple Express

part-time observer that wouldn't stay there very long. We would all talk to him, and he had a job to do, we didn't have any problems with him, at least I don't remember any. Now that the Santa trucks were blowing in and out the gates it definitely caused a lot of tension, I'm sure that was the plan. There was some real close calls where violence could have broke out. Looking back many times, it was really a stroke of luck that it didn't happen. They (the management) would love for us out on the picket line, to act real stupid, get into some kind of a hassle, and bring negative attention to us. It was really hard to walk away from. One particular instant Bobby and I had a confrontation with a Santa driver that still sticks out in my mind. A testy period that was hard to swallow, for sure!

I stayed at the Spokane street plant all thru the strike, and one of the few times I ventured over to the main plant to see what was going on, I had a few humorous moments with an incident while I was there. We had this one driver Frank S., he was known as a political activist. I use to talk with Frank all the time but he ran in different circles than I did. I liked Frank, for some reason, he said a lot of things I thought were funny. He had an entertaining effect on me, don't know why but he did. At the main plant, the warehouse section was a couple hundred feet south of the batch plant up a slight concrete little alley, I guess that's the way to describe it. There was an office on one side and the shops on the other. They had the picket line set up outside the warehouse office and the people were sitting around in lawn chairs with picket signs. Outta the blue... Frank comes roaring down the little alley in a 1963 Chevy, gets into the main yard, does a 180, like in an action movie, makes the 180 like an accomplished stunt man, he nails it to the wood and comes roaring out past the audience (us). I was cracking up so hard my sides were hurting again. It was completely unexpected, and really entertaining. It just so happened that, this trucking outfit from Everett, that had steady hauls from Lone Star just happened to cross the picket line for a load while I was there. I said, "Those guys are union aren't they?" Yes they were, and I spoke up and said, "Why are they getting Lone Star business?"

I still had friends over at System Transfer. Their salesman Joe Salvatore was a friend of mine and I looked him up. I said "Joe, as soon as this strike is over, why don't you pay the warehouse a visit and see if you guys can get some business, it's there", and I explained the union trucking outfit crossing the line. When the strike ended, Joe did go to the warehouse, he was able to secure some business, he thanked me, and I felt pretty good about the whole thing. Meanwhile... the strike is still in progress and there would be some more events worth mentioning.

A short time before the strike, Lone Star had hired a low management guy named Mike P. As I have traveled thru life from the time I can remember, all the adult men in my life as parents, teachers, and mentors all pounded into my head, "be a man". I especially remember the Priests we had in high school that expected you to know that. After high school and in the Military for 4 years, it goes without saying what was expected of you. BE A MAN! So, when people come into my life in any form and try to be telling me what to do, I approach from the standpoint of a man and I expect other men to deal with me on that level. I can say in all honesty, I may not like you personally, but, if you deal with me in an honorable way, I will still respect you and that is all I ask. So... Lone Star brought this guy Mike P in to be a management type guy and I could see thru this shallow punk from day one. He immediately started doing the demoralizing things guys like that do for their show of power. Telling drivers to take their AM radios out of their trucks. The mixer I drove was so old it didn't have a radio in it, but it was this kind of crap the guy was dishing out. It didn't take long for him to get his nick name "The Weasel", that's the way most of the drivers called him behind his back. The weasel was one of the regulars at the Spokane street strike and I was almost positive he was the one to encourage bringing in the Santa trucks to cross the picket lines. He lived on the east side and he knew Santa.

I actually knew Santa myself. He wasn't a friend of mine. In 1975, he had called me where I lived and asked me to come to work on a job out in Issaquah driving belly dump. It would be

The Cool Apple Express

known as "The Hi Point Job", a huge fill job. He was operating as a union company then, and he had told me he had a big fill job but was having trouble getting good drivers. I did not know the man before he called me. I don't even remember how he actually found out about me. He knew Rocky and I were close friends; he wanted to know if I could get him and brother Bob to come out there too. I told him they were both running the Al-Can, but, I would let them know as soon as I saw them. I went out there and drove about 2 months till he bought a fleet of worn out rigs from some logging outfit in Oregon, and I said "no thanks, I will do my driving somewhere else". That was just before I went to work at C F Tank lines. While I was out on the picket line, he came to the gate and said hi to me. The first thing he said was, "where's Rocky?". I asked him what he was doing screwing with the working man. He gave me some song & dance B S and I kept the conversation to a minimum. I was looking up into the tower at the time and the "weasel" was watching that little interaction very intently. Some events would follow, that would confirm my suspicions of his connections with the weasel.

After many weeks, and with a lot of new strains to deal with now, the strike finally came to an end. For me personally, there would be hard feelings that would last the rest of the time at Lone Star, unfortunately. Head games, power trips, and demoralization attitudes would be management's way of dealing with the situations to come. We were coming into the slowest time of the year for work and they were able to milk that bigtime, especially to punish people with low seniority. I was one of them. We're into the fall of 1980 and for the rest of that year and all of 1981, things were kind of rocky for a while, but when the work picks up, that stuff kind of takes a back seat, there's work to do, not that it is going to go away completely. I have to think while all this time is passing, the weasel is scheming in his warped little mind of how he can make things hard on me.

1982 started out great, I took a week of vacation and went to the Rose Bowl. Huskies performed the first shut-out in 30 years beating Iowa 28-O. I drove up to Sepulveda and visited my Uncle Frank while I was in Southern Cal., I hadn't seen him since I was a kid. That would be the last time I would ever see Frank alive again. We had a nice visit for about 4 hours and he seemed the very same as I had remembered him as a kid. Uncle Frank was a guy with a lot of class, like everyone in his family had, and he was complaining about restaurants in Sepulveda having topless waitresses. I was in for a surprise when I got back to work.

The weasel's 2nd office was the cocktail lounge just past the Lone Star warehouse. As far as I knew, all the people at the warehouse were friendly's for me. One of the guys, came up to me one morning shortly after the first of the year and said, "Mike I got something for you, and I been saving it till I could give it to you in person". He handed me this hand written note to read. It had been drafted by the weasel, in the cocktail lounge, obviously. I read the note, and it was pretty caustic and aimed at me personally. He had dropped the note in the parking lot just past the warehouse, probably half-drunk before he got into his car to drive where ever he was going. The warehouse guy, and I won't use his name, he and I discussed this note, and he told me he hoped I would go to the Union on this asshole. So I was warned, and I kept the note, and sure enough, the weasel was out to stir up trouble for me bigtime.

In all of my adult life, one of my largest assets has been, my work ethic, how much effort I put into doing a good job, I can honestly say, I don't know anyplace I have ever worked, that would try to incorporate bad work performance on me into some kind of a way to put me in a bad light no matter how bad they might not like me. People can and have thoughts of me being an asshole, or didn't like the way I looked, or were jealous of something, or were threatened by me in some way. So when this letter came down to me from Lone Star on 13 January 1982, and it contained the words... "Refusal to follow instructions and your continual harassment of... personnel." I wanted to fight! I wanted to fight! To me, this ranks on the same level as a woman charging me with rape, and it never happened. I write about that in an early chapter. I sent two letters, one to the

The Cool Apple Express

Weasel, and one to the head of the Seattle area Lone Star facilities. I filed a Grievance with the Union. The head of Lone Star at that time sent me a letter and it said," I am withdrawing the warning letter I issued you on January 13th."To anyone that dislikes unions, this is a perfect example of why unions were originally established. I should never have had to go to the union for help. The whole story was a concocted lie to deliberately discredit me, stir up trouble and put me in a bad light. I saved all the papers from that event in my safe for all these years. I stayed at Lone Star for another year and a half. They continued to try to create a situation at times that was to stir things up for me, I handled it pretty well most of the time and boy it was hard to suck up some times. One day Stan B must have been feeling his oats and decided to have a confrontation in the dispatch tower. I told him to get his ass out on the railroad tracks and he could show me what he was made of. He immediately called the Union and asked for a business agent to come over, Mike Hicks a driver, had invited him outside. The business agent showed up, and he handled it very good. I didn't know the guy at that time, he was part of the brand new union administration and I did get to know him after that. It was shortly after that, that I figured it was time for me to get out of there. I didn't want to give up 4 years seniority, and the business agent didn't want me to either, but I did, and I found some pretty good work to tie me over till I could find a good job. All the time I was at Lone Star I didn't put a scratch on a piece of equipment. I took care of everything I drove, and drove everything the proper way. They were real glad to have me when I first came there because I could drive everything there. Less than a year after I left, Lone Star was bought out and I was told by friends of mine still working there, they all had to be re-hired again. What?? That's what I was told. I can only imagine if I had held out and had to go thru that. It would never fly.

POST LONE STAR THE NEXT 3 YEARS AND SANITY

I HAVE INTENTIONALLY LEFT out a big responsibility I had in conjunction with everything else I did, work, love life, hobbies, adventures, etc., and that was, I had been looking after my mother since 1977. She was diagnosed with TERMINAL CANCER in March 1977. I was working at System Transfer at the time. She had the same Doctor since 1947, a really great guy named John Angus Clark. He looked her in the eye and told her she had 6 months to live. That would probably work with a lot of people, but my Mother was in complete shock. I was the only immediate family she had in the whole world. Mom and I had a raft of problems between us when I was growing up and really didn't become that close until I had come back from Texas in 1965 when I was 27 years old. We became good friends and we still had problems with her bouts of drinking. Anyway... I was the only one to be there for her and she leaned on me as heavy as a person could. I really don't know what came over me, but, something inside me got a grip that would never let go, and it directed me to take care of her the rest of her life. In the beginning we were planning for her to only live 6 months, that's what her Doctor said. Events would transpire to change all that and she would actually live another 22 years. It was a rocky, rocky road, and for me personally, it was a second job that would never end. So… when I had all these difficulties at work, or any other problems to deal with, I always had the 7 day a week job of looking after Mom. I tried like hell to not bring it up in my work place and I imagine a lot of people never even knew what was happening behind the green door. I kept her in her house and took care of both her and her house. I had my own place to take care of along with everything else in my life. It was always a long day.

I have to explain how she came to have Doctor Clark because, it wasn't under normal circumstances, and many years later he would play a part in one of my embarrassing moments. It was 1947 and I was 9 years old. The drinking and the parties that went on in the living room of our little house behind the store, in WWII, they could have easily made a movie out of that. My real Dad was in the Marine Corps and he was away from all of this, but my Mother had met a soldier stationed in Seattle, he was from "Hell's Kitchen" in New York city. They got married in 1943, he got a 30 day furlough and they split for New York for their honeymoon. Every bit of free time in Seattle, there were service men at the house and it was a constant party going on. Unfortunately for my Mother, this heavy drinking along with a physically, and traumatic breakup between my Mother and her 2nd husband, just after the end of WWII in late 1945, would be a bane for her existence for many years afterwards. My Mother was 8 months pregnant, they were drinking heavily, my step dad picked her up, tossed her through a plate glass window onto the front porch; dragged her back into the house; shoved her under the 1916 Stark upright player piano, and took off in my Grandpa's 41 Chevy with another woman. My Mother would be in the hospital for an entire month and of course the baby was dead. My step dad didn't do one day behind bars for that little dust up.

So… My Mother was a hard worker but she had a drinking problem that went on for decades afterwards. On a particular day in 1947, I was in immediate attendance, my Mother was wandering around the house and it was eerie. She was talking to imaginary people, and acting super strange. I told Grandpa, and brought one of the neighbors in. To get to the point, SHE HAD THE D T's! They called a Doctor in White Center, Doctor Clark, and Doctors made house calls in those days. I was there the whole time, and Doctor Clark showed up at the house for the first time in his life to tend to my Mother whom he met for the first time in his, and her life. I'm now 72 years old, was 9 back then, and the whole situation was so profound, it's still etched in my brain. As experienced as the Doctor might have been back then, I don't think he was prepared for what he had on his hands once he got there. He, in his own ad libed way, performed a medical exorcism on my Mother. It was another one of those things that would be talked about in my little family, and close friends for years. My Mother thought the world of Doctor Clark after that, and would go to him for anything she was worried about over any other Doctor.

I got to know Doctor Clark but I only remember two times in all the years he was connected to the family, that I called on him. He had me in the hospital overnight one time when he cut this thing out of the arch of my foot that was a suspected ganglion. It turned out that it wasn't, and that was in 1975 I think. But wait... there's more! In 1973, when I was running the Coast for ONC Alfreight, I had a problem that was real private and I felt comfortable only going to see Doctor Clark. I had met this woman in Phoenix, and I was doing a pattern of trips then. I would get a load going to somewhere in California, and then I would get runs between LA & Phoenix for about 10 days before I would get a load home to Seattle. This woman I met had a mobile home and I would spend nights there when I was passing through. We were having some pretty heavy duty sex at the time, and obviously I was just one guy in the chow line, and then... I got this problem with my plumbing. I went to see Doctor Clark. He checked me out and said, "You got the Love Bug Mick!" He pumped me full of penicillin, and sent me out the door with a big bottle of it to keep swallowing until they were all gone. I went over to my Mothers; stayed in the back bedroom for about 4 days out of sight. When I figured things had cleared well enough for me to resume life, I got a load and headed out of town. Doctor Clark was not only a great man, but he sure had to treat the people in my family for off the wall problems!

The union business agent that was called to Lone Star by Stan B., he kept a watch on me immediately after I pulled the pin there. He was aware of what I had been dealing with and I know he felt like he could probably put himself in my shoes. His name was Rod, and even though I was not personally endorsing the new Union administration, I liked Rod, he was making an honest effort to be in my corner and I respected him for that. He called me at home a couple times right after I left Lone Star with some tips for part time driving. They paid off in the short term and I took advantage of them. I hauled lumber between two completely different trucking companies. It was what it was, casual working always entails being used with the thought today is your last day. Life has never been a smooth road for Mike Hicks since the day I could remember, and that is why I'm writing this book. I learned at a very early age, it didn't do any good to whine and snivel about things, you just had to suck it up and try to get by or do better. Maybe things don't happen to me any different than other people, but I've been told so many times, "Mike, things like this don't happen to other people". Who knows?

Right away, I got in with these two different places, both hauling lumber. I was on call with both and it was working out pretty well, when one was busy, the other wasn't and vice versa. Most of the trips were way freighting lumber north to the Canadian border. There could be 12 stops to make and side trips thru Whidbey Island to different lumber distributors, or yards. I really liked it and so did the regular guys, and I knew it was a seasonal thing, a casual job.

On one particular trip, I noticed the steering on the tractor I was driving didn't feel right. We were always maxed out for weight and on this trip I was running the sharp turns on Whidbey going into Oak Harbor. When I got back in to Seattle that night, I knew the steering should be looked at. I mentioned it to one of the regular

The Cool Apple Express

guys and his comment was, "Ah, there's probably nothing wrong, I drive that unit all the time, if you think it needs work, take it out to Freightliner". I took it to Freightliner and left it overnight. The next day I checked on the equipment, Freightliner said, "Of the 4 bolts to hold the steering box in place, 3 were gone with only 1 bolt securing the entire unit". Nobody said a whole lot about it, but being an outsider that was driving there, I felt like I knew what I was doing and was REALLY glad as hell I put it in the shop.

I had been looking at a few places to work steady and one of them was SeaBay, they were a part of the Seattle Disposal complex. They were local, hauled solid waste out of town to the landfills, not necessarily a pretty job but, a good paying Union job and there is always going to be solid waste to get rid of. I went over there several times while I was still working part time hauling lumber. I got to know the guy to see, Dale L., I told him all about my trucking experience and also everything that took place at Lone Star. I didn't have anything to hide about what took place at Lone Star and we even talked about it in depth a little. One day in September 1983, Dale L gave me a call and asked me if I wanted to come in for a day's work, and I jumped on it. He was as nice as he could be and it was a real good feel again. He had me get a particular tractor to do the job I was assigned to do. I popped the cap on the fuel tank and it was full to the top. Now, there were two fuel tanks on the tractor and I didn't worry about having enough fuel. I don't remember exactly what I was doing, I think I was just hauling containers off the piers, but I ran outta fuel. I was stunned! I called in and Dale was nice as hell, he came out and rescued me with some fuel till we could get it into the yard and top it off. The story goes like this. Many tractors in that fleet have 2 saddle tanks, like a lot do. In this case, one tank is used for diesel fuel to run the equipment and the other tank was used for hydraulic fuel to run all the power on the trash trailers that would normally be hauled behind to the landfill. I had no way of knowing that. When I checked the one tank, and it was full to the top, that tank was hydraulic fuel and to me, thinking it was diesel was a normal thing. Dale said, no problem, but I still felt stupid. So… if it can happen, it can happen to me, and it did. Dale kept me fairly busy for a while and I was an outsider, there was no immediate hiring situation, and if I wanted to get on steady, I just had to ride that horse wherever it went. We got into early winter and I was barely working. I may have been getting some week-end work at Burlington Northern where I hauled containers and pigs on the week-ends for years. So things were slow now, and I would supplement this down time by finding a car to fix up and sell.

Things were real slow for a couple months and I was kind of getting the feeling I might be passed over and then… It was in March I got a call from Dale and he said, "We're bringing you in Mike and you will be working steady now." That was a breath of fresh air. So things would be a little different now. I was going to be hauling solid waste to the landfill full time and by- pass the container hauling. I made a few trips with "Sweet Al" to get the feel of the route, what to do at the landfill, how to run the decks on the trailer to off load the garbage. I had known Al from the very first I ever got into trucking in Seattle, not very well, just on sight mostly. He was another one of those local legends in Seattle trucking. He had worked at the Taylor-Edwards warehouse, I think, for about 30 years. Anybody hauling freight around Seattle would eventually get to un-load at Taylor—Edwards. When I talked to him for a while, he told me he had been working at System, but walked away from there when SeaBay called. I think he said System still wanted him back. I remember back in time one day, I took a one day job out of the hall. I had to pick up this trailer, I think it was at Trans-Con, and take it into Taylor- Edwards and off load it. When I opened the doors, that trailer was stuffed, wall to wall, floor to ceiling, it had one zillion small cases and they all had to be un-loaded, and palletized. I was there about 7 hours. It's funny how you never forget these types of situations.

So now I'm working every day and shortly after that I was put on a 4-10 shift strictly hauling to the land fill. We had two, one for demolition, which was the "Coal Creek', dump near Cougar Mountain, and the "Cedar Hills" dump, run by King County, that is

The Cool Apple Express

where the standard garbage was dumped. At that time. The "Coal Creek" dump was a challenge for a lot of reasons. Getting in and getting dumped without getting stuck in the mud, and getting out without a flat tire. You can bet you are going to have a flat tire at least 50% of the time you go in there. It was a real challenge to watch for the cat driver, he would point to where you were to dump. All this time, you didn't want your rig to stop moving. You would eyeball the spot, engage the interlock, keep it moving, this all done of course after you had climbed the hill, stopped somewhere at the top to examine the rear doors, keep it moving and then start the floor of the trailer moving. If you could get thru that quagmire, have the trailer emptied and make it thru without getting stuck, that's a touchdown, 6 points. Sometimes it would be pouring rain, you're stuck in the middle of the mire, you motion for the driver on the cat to come over and pull you free. You had to get out of the cab… you're gonna be in a minimum of a foot of muck. He throws you the steel cable and you latch on to the hook under your bumper and he pulls you free. It was part of the job. Just hope by the time you got off the hill and down to the asphalt, your bogies (wheels) had discarded the major mud and it's not flying off in chunks. It would get 100% better later on down the road when the company I worked for bought that entire area, cleaned it up, brought in real good equipment and ran it in a disciplined manner. Years down the road they would turn that land fill into one of the most luxurious golf courses in the state of Washington.

In the fall of 1984, they took me off the garbage haul for a short time. I was making two trips to Spokane every week hauling full trailer loads of bundled re-cycled newspapers to a company that used it to make insulation. I would go up to Fairchild Air Force Base and load up re-cycled cardboard back to Seattle. On hump day (Wednesday) I would be in Seattle and haul garbage that day. Tarp and tie down my second load to Spokane before I went home. I laid over in Spokane on Monday and Thursday nights. I really liked that run, but it didn't last that long. Winter came early that year and I had some fun on a couple of those trips. One trip, I was just barley ahead of an early winter storm. As I was climbing Snoqualamie, the ground blizzard had begun. It was the week of elk season and a lot of hunters on the move too. As soon as I got over the pass the temp was dropping fast and it was snowing real hard. When I got into Spokane it was in the mid 20's, but the wind was blowing like hell. I had to roll my tarps, the concrete and asphalt was already iced over real good. I finally got the tarps rolled and headed up to Fairchild to get the back load. Up at Fairchild they told me no way. They weren't going to let a forklift driver onto my trailer in these weather conditions. I went back into Spokane and got a room where I usually stayed. I called a local broker and wanted to know if he could get me a load to Seattle. Problem solved! He had a load I could get early the next morning about 18 miles east of Spokane at a brick plant. They had a full load going about 6 blocks away from where I worked. Tooooo Sweeeet! Not only that, I was going to have one solid load going back in all that shitty weather.

When I went to bed it was 10 degrees outside, several inches of snow on the ground, the forecast was more of the same. Wrong! I was up early and during the nite the wind had shifted.

It was still cold, right about 32 degrees, but nothing like when I went to bed. It was actually raining, about half freezing rain, and it was a mess. I drove out to the brick plant and got squared away with the load. I felt blessed to get this square, heavy load to take back, for driving purposes.

Once I got going I was listening closely to road conditions along the way. First report said they were chaining up in Ellensburg. When I got to George, they were chaining up in CleElum. When I passed Ellensburg they were chaining up at Easton. When I got to Easton they were chaining up just a few mile before the start up the pass, and that's where I had to pull over and chain. The road was packed with trucks and a car load of punks was buzzing the truckers and peppering them with ice balls as they were chaining. Flames were coming out of my eyes and ears. I chained, pulled out into the procession and it was really slow going. That wasn't the shocker. Looking at the traffic headed east bound was the shocker.

The Cool Apple Express

I found out a little later, they had shut the pass down east bound not long after I had gotten over the day before. Horror stories about the traffic that had been backed up all that time. There was about 14 inches of snow on the road as I dropped off, and when I got to the bottom at Denny Creek, I took the off ramp and pulled over. Stepping out into that deep, wet slush to drag the chains off, and then run er on in. Traffic east bound was still backed up all the way to North Bend. I had it real easy compared to those guys.

I had a couple more rough trips on that run during the early winter, but they shut that haul down completely and I was never told why. I was back on the garbage haul full time again and it would turn out that the winter of 84/85 would be a cold and snowy winter for the tenderfoots like us on the west side too.

While I was on that run to Spokane, I had said earlier, that I would spend Wednesday in Seattle hauling to the landfills, and then tarp my Thursday load before going home. On one particular Wednesday, I had the tractor of one of the special people that drove at SeaBay. I call him special people because, he had a special tractor, and they had him doing special jobs. I had seen the guy around for years, he had driven for Maust for a long time, but he never talked to me much, and I don't remember his name. He had this International tractor he drove, the only one like it in the fleet. It was powered real good, and they had me drive it one day. At that particular time, we were having some trouble out at Cedar Hills and I never fully understood the political in-fighting that went on in the companies. We were being squeezed at the dump site for a descent place to dump and it was causing some problems. The Cat operator had actually threatened some of the drivers with bodily harm and we were having to try to get our loads off in a really tight area, and drive out. This special tractor I was driving on this particular Wednesday was nice to drive but it had the craziest steering system ever. It would turn normal to the right, but a lot shorter to the left. The area they were making us dump in was not being taken care of properly, solid objects were not graded, the muck was worse than where the County was dumping because they wouldn't spread any rock thru our area. On this one pass I was making thru this spot with a full load, I had to cut it sharp to the left and dump at the same time, we just had a real tight spot to dump in. There was no way to see the lurking hazard I was about to encounter. A bed spring, sticking up out of the mire, grabbed my drive line while I'm moving, and wrapped itself around the U-joint about twenty times, and I was dead in the landfill. I got into the yard on a radio, and help was immediately on the way. The truck boss came out with a Polaroid camera and took a bunch of pictures of the mess. I think that was the straw that broke the camel's back because, the County immediately took a different approach to us coming out there by giving us more space, and grading, putting down rock in our dump area. The company didn't give me any static about the situation but, the special driver, for the special tractor I was driving, wanted his tractor back, and I know he didn't want me to drive it. No big thing, but some good came out of the situation, dumping from then on was a whole lot better.

It was early in December of 1984 and I started having some real strange symptoms in my head, flu like, causing some severe weakness. The weather was bad naturally, that time of the year. I had a 6:30AM start, and that meant I needed to be moving my rig forward at 6:30 sharp, which I did every morning. Well… this sickness that was upon me was ripping me off so bad, it was all I could do to get up at 4 and get my butt down to work. I went into the Doctor and had a big exam and he couldn't find anything. I kept working every work day and it was a real drag. The Huskies were going to be playing in the Orange Bowl, I had planned a week's vacation during the Holidays so I could go down to Miami, but I hadn't got my ticket yet. I was trying to hide this sickness I had because, to me it would be a sign of weakness and I didn't want to draw attention to me that way. When Christmas week-end had arrived I was really sick. I should have never been out there driving in that crummy weather, to this day, there are a lot of blank spots because, I was out there driving on instincts just trying to get thru the day.

The Cool Apple Express

The good news was, I had a week off, the bad news, I just collapsed into bed and would stay there for an entire week. I hadn't got my ticket or reservations to go to the Orange Bowl, and it would have been money down the drain, I was just too wiped out. That whole week Emily looked after me and if it hadn't been for her, lord only knows where I would have been. I can say this now, that period I was sick, and it totaled about 2 months, was the sickest I have ever been in my entire life. When it came time to go back to work, I don't remember if I went back then, or took another week off. I do know there was another entire week in there somewhere, that I stayed home in bed all week again, and that would be a week without pay. The Doctor ran a complete test on me again, it was obvious something was wrong. They still couldn't pin it down, but something showed up as a virus in my system and so the Doctor turned it over to a specialist at the old Northgate Hospital. The Doctor escorted me to the other Doctor and stayed the whole time I was at that appointment. They took me in this semi dark room with indirect lighting. I sat in a chair something like a barber or dentist chair. I got a glimpse of the 2nd Doctor with a syringe in his hand with a needle about 3 feet long. It wasn't something I was real thrilled about, but I was so sick and so weak, I almost didn't give a damn by this time. The two Doctors were both talking, they were trying to critique me on what was going to take place. I don't really remember what they told me, but I do remember the words, "we will be putting the syringe into your nasal passage", and the one Doctor did. I can't say this definitely, but I am sure the Doctor shot steroids into my sinuses on both sides. It was a little painful, but not the worst I had ever endured. If it worked it would be worth it.

About 48 hours after the medical procedure things started happening. Looking back, things would start to improve from that point on, but it was not an overnite sensation. It would be weeks before I would get anywhere close to normal. I had been so sick, I was at the bottom of the barrel, and up was the only direction I could go. I was out there every day driving my unit, dealing with the winter weather along with trying to make headway with this virusX that had wacked me. I would be driving along on the job and I would get these weird sensations in my scalp. I guess it was around February before I could say I was close to normal, but it took a long time after that before I would get my strength back and I worked real hard on getting that done. I remember we had a lot of snow, and cold weather to deal with during that period of time, but the clarity is scrambled, all I can say is, I was sick as hell and just trying to survive.

We're into 1985 now and it's pretty much a groove type thing with week in week out work. I bought a house in Northgate in October and moved in. I would wind up living in that little house on 5th NE for exactly 18 years. It was one of the best moves I ever made in my life. In December, I collected money from the immediate group of working people I was around and we had a Christmas Party at "Lofurnos". Everybody had a great time and talked about the party for a long time. They wanted to do it again the next year.

A good time to describe the immediate body of people I worked with at SeaBay. There were no evil people working there to my knowledge. It was as about as perfect a cross section of blue collar people you could ever ask for. Outsiders might stick up there nose at the type of work we did, in relation to garbage, but in the big picture, it was a good job without a lot of fanfare, and any flaws in the system, on a personal level, were just normal. You can have arguments in your own family, and any arguments that would take place there were not necessarily out of hatred, just disagreements and normal misunderstandings. Hell, I can remember a Christmas Eve in our house in 1947, I was 9 years old. A fist fight broke out in our kitchen, right in front of me. One minute everyone was celebrating, (way too much booze), the next second, Charlie and Bob were going full tilt at each other. They were both big guys, both truck drivers and that kitchen was very small. A lot of dukes were thrown, and Bob's head went thru a door window cutting a vein in his neck. They rushed him up to Harborview, and there was blood all over the kitchen. It was a story that would be talked about for decades in my family. It happened

The Cool Apple Express

63 years ago, and I can remember it just like it was yesterday. Needless to say, That Christmas was not the greatest Holiday to remember. The people weren't evil, but there was an argument, and s... happened. Another thing that was happening every day at SeaBay, among the people I worked with back then, was race relations were just about as good as you would ever find in America. It wasn't forced, it just worked out that way. There was a large percentage of blacks working there, and for the most part, things were harmonious. I thought we got along great, when you consider at this particular time I'm writing this book, race is in the headlines every day. It wasn't like we had to have sensitivity training, or, there was some kind of a diversity specialist, or there were people coming up with selective outrage, we were a workforce that got paid good wages and handled things that seem to come out right. There were some very heated arguments, and I was involved in 2 memorable ones, one especially at my departure, but it was a plain ole disagreement between two white guys, and sometimes you just have to suck things up even if they aren't fair in their outcome. It happened in my case, I wish it hadn't, it did, I had to handle the best way I could, and I did.

While I was driving fulltime at SeaBay, I had a hand in teaching two different people how to drive, that would ultimately become full time drivers there. One named Wes, the other one I think his name was Rick. I remember a lot of times when I first came back to Seattle in 1965, and how I did all that side saddle learning from Rocky, Bob, Craig and few others. I was fortunate to learn from fanatics, it really paid off in the overall picture of things I would have to deal with. I wasn't quite the fanatic of the teachers I had, but I was specific about learning how to do it right, and I know I did a good job in teaching others to drive the right way.

In 1986, SeaBay bought a couple brand new Peterbilt's equipped with the new 3406B Cat engine. These were great!! I didn't get one, they went to guys with top seniority, but I did get to test drive one and I fell in love with that Cat engine immediately. From the beginning of my trucking career, I was taught to like the Cummins engine, and it became a theme with me, that I only wanted to drive Cummins. Of course, I would have to drive whatever I was assigned where ever I worked. I couldn't believe my own self, how I fell in love with that Cat engine so well, so fast. One morning, the company brought Cat instructors out to work, and all the drivers went to Cat school for 3 hours. It also was great, and informative. I would go on to put a lot of miles on the 3406B Cat over the next several years, and that little 3 hour school, with all the basics to know about that engine, really paid off down the road too. A little later on in that year, they did a complete overhaul on my tractor, tying it up for over 2 months. During that period of time, I would have to take whatever I could get my hands on to drive my first 3 days that week, but on the 4th day, Friday, the regular driver of one of the new Pete's had Friday off, and I would drive his unit that day. Finished off my week in good shape. The 3406B Cat engine was the best engine I ever had the pleasure of driving. Some years later when I was driving for the Boeing Co., the 3406B Cat engine wound up being the major engine used in most of the tractors.

My Exit from SeaBay Transportation

I have thought long and hard how I would write this section in my book. It is important for me to get everything right here for a lot of reasons. My story was never told because, I was absent for obvious reasons. I will swear before God that everything I say here is the absolute truth.

I was working a 4-10 shift, Tuesday thru Friday. It must have started on Monday of the week, 7 December 1986. My dog Vantage was real sick and she was staying at my Mothers. It was real cold, in the mid 30's, raining, my Mom called me. She said Vantage wouldn't stay inside, she wanted to lay in the rain under the tree outside. I think her shoulder was burning up. Early Monday morning I took her to the Vet in Northgate. He told me he couldn't save her, she had a big cancer in her shoulder. She had to be put to sleep. I had a 5 pound ball in my throat. I said, O K, but I'm going to hold her when you put the needle in her leg. Here's a

The Cool Apple Express

muscled up 190 pound man, holding his dog, crying his eyes out while she is put to sleep. The Vet asked me if I wanted him to dispose of her and I said no, I'll take her with me. I took her home, got me a shovel and went into the backyard. I started digging in that hardpan, screaming with every shovel load, sometimes I had tears in my eyes. I got the grave dug, put her in it, and that would be the beginning of an unforgettable week.

Vantage was 13 years old, I had found her at the very same time of the year. I would pull extra trips for Bestway back in the early winter of 1973, do a Vantage turn. Take a fully loaded set of doubles to the bottom of Vantage, take the last ramp across to the uphill side, there was a huge barren space. Wait for a set coming in from Spokane with a load of sailboat fuel. It was a cold, raw nite, wind blowing down the Columbia. I saw this real young puppy running around outside. There were no visible buildings anywhere, have no idea where she came from. I went outside, picked her up, brought her inside my cabover Kenworth and put her on the nice warm doghouse next to the driver's seat. She went directly to sleep, unlike a hyper puppy would. When the driver arrived from Spokane, we swapped sets, and I was on my way back to the Emerald city.

I always lived in an apartment in those days, and I took the dog to Mom's and the rest was history. That dog bonded with me more than any living thing on this earth ever did. I did a lot of running in those days and that dog would rather run than eat when she got grown. If I even looked like I was going to run, she made sure we were joined at the hip. I can remember about a year later, I was up on Nason Creek camping out with a girlfriend. We stayed up there for 5 days and we lived like we were a thousand miles from anywhere. Vantage was there every step of the way swimming, running and hiking. It was great. No downside to anything. It was really painful to part with her. I've had dogs ever since I was a kid and every one of them was real close to me, but for some reason, Vantage was at another level being bonded with me. She would stick with me like glue, and where ever we went or whatever we did, she always minded me and was the perfect companion for a dog.

So the week is starting out on a low note, to say the least, and for some reason I can't explain, it would be the same at work before the week was over. The truck boss had been gone for almost a month, and it had to do with the Peterbilt sponsored race car owned by the company. That was really irrelevant to anything I had to do at work except, with him gone, we garbage haulers were pretty much left on our own to show up for work and perform our duties as drivers without having to be told what to do. Not a problem, it was a mentality that was in place most of the time anyway, and that was one of the beauties of working there, I always thought. Especially now, we were definitely making our own decisions, the guy running the containers could be asked questions since he was really the only boss to ask. He would pitch in his two bits, but, I think for the most part, he knew we had a grip and unless there was some kind of a problem, he let us do our thing.

So, this particular week seemed like square pegs in round holes at every turn. I'm sure it was the Friday of that particular week. For several weeks, up to that point, I had been using one of the new Peterbilt tractors because, the regular driver was off that day, my tractor was being worked on, I had to put a unit together every morning the first 3 days of the work week to be able to complete my job, and in the beginning, it was a person in charge of some kind that suggested I use Rod's Pete on Fridays till my tractor was out of the shop. Besides that, Rod knew I had been driving his unit and he was fine with that. I was getting ready to make my last haul of the day, had gotten the trailer loaded, was parked outside the office with the engine idling, and made a trip into the dispatch to say something I don't even remember what it was. The dispatch was kind of split between two adjoining rooms, and I was going into the far room to say something to the container dispatcher. As I was passing thru the first room, I saw our truck boss sitting there for the first time in about 4 weeks. He looked up at me as I passed, I looked down at him, I have no idea what we said to each other at that moment. I do know it was Friday, I was probably in a hurry to get that load on the road, not waste much time knowing

The Cool Apple Express

the traffic on Friday can get like hell. I said a few words to the container dispatcher, did a U-turn and was headed back to my tractor. As I passed by the desk where the truck boss was sitting, he says in a very sarcastically way, "I see you're dispatching now! "Like I had pointed out earlier, all of us had basically been doing our own dispatching the whole time he was gone except for permission to do things out of the ordinary. I stopped in front of his desk, and the conversation went from me trying to be low key to, "you got an attitude problem Mike". And more name calling from the truck boss... I said you are embarrassing me, let's go outside and you can tell me why you are saying all these things. I've had years and years to think about this and why what was about to transpire. Just a year before, I had collected money from my immediate co-workers to have a Christmas Party. The party came off great and some of them kept telling me now, they wanted to do it again. I found out shortly after that, the company wasn't happy with me about that. It brought no negative reflection on the company, I didn't understand that position. So... now it's that time of the year again and "Junior" Brown approached me and said, "Mike, we have this big chunk of salvage steel, we can take the money from that and put it into a Christmas Party, if you want to do that". I acknowledged that, but here's what I think happened. I think the people upstairs got wind of that, told the truck boss to ignite a fire in me, knowing what my response might be, and that would give them the opportunity to fire me, and put an end to any Christmas Party

We both went out the door, me first. I think this might have been thought out before hand by the truck boss, I was kind of doing things by instincts at that point, and I had stepped outside many times before in my life, I had in the back of my mind I really didn't want to be doing this over a job I had no intentions of quitting. The direction of things were moving pretty fast, and when it looked to me like the guy was going to rush me and take a swing, I just punched him and knocked him on his ass. I could have leaped on him and pole axed him, he knew that, but I didn't, I thought that was going to be enough to put a stop to what had happened up to that point. No… apparently he wanted to make a fight out of it. I let him get to his feet and he came at me swinging, he may have hit me, I don't remember and it wasn't important anymore, my instincts had taken over. As he burrowed into me, I just snatched him in a headlock with the intentions of running him head first to the fresh asphalt below which was somewhere between 3 and four feet down. When I had the opportunity to do it, I hesitated because my instincts said yes and my mind said no. Of course he was struggling while I had him in a headlock and the combination of that, along with my stepping back, I didn't know it at that split second but my right tibia broke clean in half.

I guess the shock of the break in all, I was stunned even though we were on the ground and I still had the truck boss in a headlock. I only know of 2 people that observed the whole thing. One was a new hire, a welder that I really didn't know. The other person I think, was Joe Popich. Joe was half my age, we had played some softball together on the company team a year and a half before. I liked Joe, he said he was from my original neighborhood on Holden street. I'm sure it was Joe, who came up to me and said, "Mike you can't fist fight with a broken leg". It was at that point I looked at my right leg stretched out in front of me, my left leg kind a tucked backward under me. When he said my leg was broken, that's when I looked out at my right leg, tried to move it and my foot went from 3 o'clock to 9 o'clock and back. I really didn't feel any pain, but when I saw that foot going back and forth, it took the wind outta my sails. Meanwhile, thru all this, I still have the truck boss in a headlock with my right arm. Was shortly thereafter I let him go, and then, he got to his feet and started kicking me in the back of the head. I'm pretty sure it was Joe Popich, or the welder, or somebody else that grabbed him, and he stopped kicking. So here I am in a real embarrassing situation. Jesse came out of the driver's room and put a pillow down for me. The ambulance showed up and off we went to the old Northgate Hospital.

Of all people to be Doctor of the day at the Hospital, Doctor Gruber, my Doctor. He had worked on that same leg 4 years before when I stepped wrong one day hauling mud to the new West Seattle bridge. He had treated me for torn ligaments in my ankle and this break was up just a bit on the Tibia. He looked me in the eye in the E R and said, "Mike, I can throw a cast on it and not guarantee it will come out perfect, or, I can do surgery, put an open cast on it, and if you follow my rules, you will come out fine." Do the surgery!

The nest day, Doctor Gruber did 3 hours of surgery on my leg, put in an 8 inch plate with 8 screws. His workmanship in the long run turned out great, of all my injuries, that one rehabbed the best. In all honesty, there was pain to deal with and mostly because I tried to move around too much once I was on crutches, but compared to all the pain I was promised, it didn't turn out to be as bad as I thought. I rehabbed like I was getting ready to play in a game, but it was 6 months till the Doc allowed me to resume working. Of course I was officially fired, in fact, the day I got home from the Hospital (in there 3 days) I had a registered letter waiting for me at home telling me I had been fired for assaulting my superior. I had lots of time to talk it over with the Union, and in the very beginning, I thought I might fight for my job, the Union said they would stand behind me, but we talked it over several times, and I decided I would wing it and let sleeping dogs lie, and that's what I did.

People that really know me, they know that everything I said is the gospel truth. With all the faults I might have, lying has never been one of them. Most of the stories that worked their way back to me after the dust settled, were all over the map. There were probably a lot that I never heard, but there was one that sticks out in my mind. Not long after this all took place, the Union business agent called me at home. He told me in his own words, "Mike, I know you won't believe this but, somebody said you were coming down to SeaBay with a 45." I was totally stunned that somebody could concoct a story and actually put it out. I would have hoped, that I had enough friends working there that wouldn't believe a lie like that. The business agent and I discussed the whole thing, and that was one of the reasons the Union really got behind me when we started discussing me fighting for my job. They told me, in the very beginning, because of what they were told, I was on thin ice as having a platform to stand on. Stories like the 45, and a little research that showed I was a well thought of employee, and thought of highly for my driving skills, the entire attitude towards me took a very visible change, and I guess you would have to say for me anyway, it was a consolation prize. Never-the-less, it was decided by me, and the Union, that I would just play things from day to day and not go up against the company to get the job back. I had a job ahead of me to get the leg right, get it rehabbed, and get my butt back on the road again.

    I would have liked for that episode to not have happened, but it did. Time has a habit of making things easier in hindsight, but there was no one I worked with that I really didn't like and that went all the way to the top as far as the people I dealt with. I had to give myself a character check over the next couple of years, there were a few disappointments along the way, but in the end I passed. No real whining, that's not my style either. SeaBay in my rear view mirror.

TWO AND A HALF YEARS OF STARTING OVER

1987 STARTED OUT THE New Year as it usually does for me with a birthday. I was now 49 years old, right leg in a cast, no job and it would be awhile before I could work anyway. Another challenge to pick yourself up, dust yourself off, and start all over again. "Got to play with the hand you are dealt." It's not my nature to be shelved, and when I am in a position to have to lay low, heal thy body, that's probably the toughest thing for me to do. A longtime friend I hadn't seen in years showed up during the Holidays. He only lived little over a mile away, and had lost his job. It became a daily ritual for Craig Richards to stop by, B S, drink some wine, and play Boogie Woogie on the 1916 upright player piano that had been in the family all those years. Every day was kind of a mini party, with two guys the same age, both without jobs, making the best of things. Craig was a good guy and I met Craig the same way I met the other Craig, Craig Stewart, thru Rocky when I came back from Texas in 1965. Craig & Craig were actually in the same class for a while in high school. All three of us were the same age, and we all crossed paths when we didn't really know each other.

I bided my time and tried to do constructive things. Once I finally got smart, stayed off the crutches, propped the leg up for awhile to let it heal, the pain was a lot less. We got into February and I had adapted pretty good, was thinking about driving soon as I felt I could do it safely. Another longtime friend that lived in Riverton, Wyoming stopped by. He was bringing a semi load into Seattle, had to off load, get a load back that way. I got him a good place to park his rig in the Northgate parking lot, and he was able to stay overnight and crash. Told him how to get to Kent to unload. His wife had been a girlfriend of mine when I was still in Texas after I had gotten divorced, 1964. Gene was in the Army then, stationed in San Antonio. We all got along great. Gene's wife Jan just passed away last year, 2008, and I hadn't even seen her since 1965.

We're into February and now I'm driving my car with one leg. It wasn't a problem, and it's funny how you can adapt to a lot of things when the need and ambition to do so is there. Dr. Gruber is a real hard case to get him to OK you getting off crutches. He was relentless to keep me on crutches and I'm feeling like I can do without them, but he wouldn't OK it and I just abided by his wishes. Getting into April, and I'm finally off crutches, looking for work even though the Doctor is not going to give me an OK to be back into trucking. I was still trying to lay groundwork for the future. Got word of the King County Solid Waste, posting a notice they were giving out tests for Solid waste semi drivers. A natural for me to apply for. I went down and signed up for the test, took the test, and waited a long time for an answer. They sent me a card in the mail stating I had scored 100, "No one had scored higher than you."

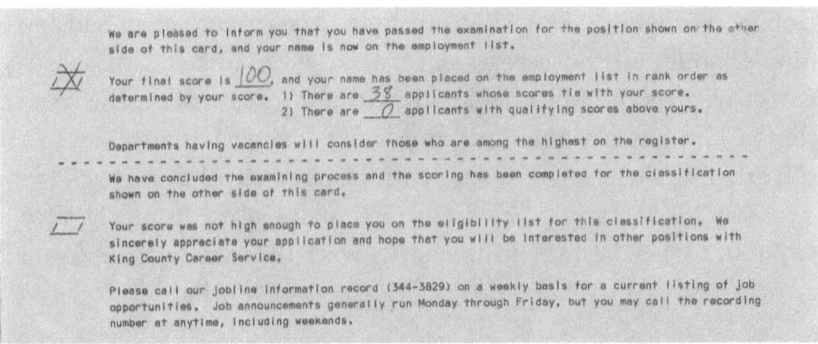

The Cool Apple Express

In the beginning, when I had first got the score back from the test, I was naturally getting a good feel about it. A while after that, the County contacted me and directed me to come out to Cedar Hills Landfill office to take an oral test, and interview. On the date specified by them, I drove out to Cedar Hills in my best blue suit. Low quarter shoes spit shinned perfectly for inspection. The perfect Windsor knot on my tie and every hair in place. When I got to the location. I recognized some of the faces from the 3 ½ years I drove in there on a daily basis dumping garbage for SeaBay. I wasn't on first name basis with anyone, I was still just another guy applying for a job. They asked me some routine questions about equipment and it's functions mostly. Then they wanted me to go outside and hook up a tractor and trailer. None of this was any kind of a a problem for me except, they had me doing this in about 3 inches of mud. I did it anyway wondering all the time, was I suppose to come out to interview for a job in Levi's and boots? When it was all over, I hopped back into my 1970 Buick Skylark, my spit shinned low quarter shoes were covered in mud clear into my socks. I thought to myself, I sure hope this is all worth the effort. I waited a long period of time for an answer, and the longer time passed, the more discouraging it got. By that time I was cleared to go back to work in June and really glad of it even though I hadn't secured a job yet.

I signed up for work at the Teamster Hiring hall and that would work out for me again for an ace in the hole as far as casual work. The dispatcher was a jewel. Arlen Overstreet would call me at home and I would make it a point to take everything she would ask me to take. Sometimes they were crummy jobs, but they paid union wages and I just put my nose to the wheel and told myself I just had to take the good with the not so good. My appreciation for Arlen asking me to work was more than I can say. If I felt she needed someone to take a particular job she might be having a hard time finding someone for, I wanted to take that job for her benefit as well as mine. There were jobs I would take for one day that would work out for 5 weeks to a couple months. It paid off!

It was long after I had taken the tests at the country before I found out thru word of mouth and not the County, they wouldn't be hiring me. It's one of those questions that will never be answered, and you just have to use your own imagination to figure out why. I know they hired mostly inexperienced young minorities and all the formalities of hiring experienced people that went by the numbers, seemed like a rouge now. What a waste of time! It did seem like a loss at the time, and part of the bumpy road, but a couple more years down the road, things would finally turn in my favor for working, and all that wouldn't mean a thing anymore.

I have to throw this one unrelated episode in here just for laughs. It was in April 1987, David Holcraft shows up at my house. He wants me to go out to the "Drift On Inn" and watch a mud wrestling match between babes. I really didn't want to go, but I gave in. In years past, I use to be one of the Romeo's that went into the "Drift On Inn" for free time, recreational activities with the opposite sex. So many times I couldn't begin to count!! We show up at the Drift, and there isn't really a lot of people there, 30 to 40 people. They had this kids pool filled with jello and the babes would get into it an wrestle. It was pretty boring stuff, but I was out, and everybody was laughing and drinking, and they had all the tables joined together stretched out the length of the dance floor with people facing each other. Dave and me sit down, and I spot this huge guy looking over at us. The first thing that comes into my mind is, I'm out of the house in a bar for the first time since I had this leg broke in half. This huge dude is looking over here and is this going to turn out to be a lot of trouble. I hope not! It wasn't, but just a few minutes after that, the huge guy talks to Dave and me and introduces himself. He told us he was Brian Millard and he had just signed with the SeaHawks. I knew who he was, he had been playing for the N J Generals in another league. He was a hell of a nice guy, and he wound up being a starter on the Offensive line for the Hawks for a long time. Happy, relieved, and ready to go home after such an exciting evening of Babe mud wrestling, I bid Dave a fond adios and headed for home.

The Cool Apple Express

It was in late June, I had Doctors permission to go to work, and I got a call from the Hall while I was working on a car in my garage. Kewitt Construction had a job on a dam out near North Bend. It was a job that started at 4PM and would go round the clock till 6 in the morning. I took it, not knowing how long it would last. They had these 8 yard mixers doing an off road job. There was no break, but they paid you for it. I felt good, but I hadn't done manual labor for 6 months and I had to get into the groove. They had me come out every afternoon for about a week, then they laid me off. The pay was excellent, and I assumed I would never see them again. Never had worked for Peter Kewitt before. I had heard there name a million times, but never worked there.

A few days after that job came to an end, Arlen at the Hall dispatched me to this driving job for a Bed company. They had a full size whoopee truck, and also a swamper to go with you. I was going to find myself doing some pretty strenuous work now with lots of hours. I would punch in between 6 and 6:30 in the morning, and lots of times we would be out there past 9 at nite. Lots of lifting, lots of lugging. Knowing the lay of the land was my biggest asset. I would do fine till we got into the fashionable east side and some crazy numbering over there. The swampers were all young hearty guys around 21 years old. That made it good when it come time to lug a heavy hide-a-bed into a multiple storied apartment. One time we had to get this King sized bed into the second story of a home. It had a staircase, narrow, that did a ninety degree turn. I know we finally got it up and put together, I don't remember how we did it. It was 10 pounds of shit in a 2 pound sack, and we busted our balls getting it in there. The job paid good, I was doing a lot of hours and the checks were nice. I must have worked there for about 2 months, maybe a little longer, it's kind of a blur at times. I don't remember why I left there, but I am sure it was because the work slowed and I fell back on the Hall because, I followed up with a job from Arlen at the Hall. A driver was going to be down with a gall bladder operation for awhile, and a local door company, Peachtree Hardwood Doors, under the Freemont bridge, needed a steady driver till he got back. Arlen wanted me to take the job if I could, and I made sure I would take care of it.

It was really a neat job. They had a solo unit that could be set up for truck- trailer, but they didn't have the trailer. It was a flat bed with a hi cube canopy with curtains. Easy to work off of, and if the weather gets nasty, pull the curtains, and tighten it down. On MWF, you run north to the Canadian border way freighting doors to lumber yards. On Tu and Thu., you run south thru the valley way freighting, and would wind up at the Harwood door yard in Tacoma. There was not one negative thing related to this job. The pay scale was a little lower but it was a steady check, knowing it was going to be steady for 5 or 6 weeks. I blended in immediately and it worked out well. Sometimes unloading a double door in an out of the way lumber yard, with out help was a little strenuous at times, but when I am happy in my work, I get er done! I was told the regular driver would be gone 5 to 6 weeks, and one Friday I came into the office after all my work was done. The regular driver was in the office and I was introduced to him. I think he said he would be back in a week or two. He showed me the long scar on his trunk from the surgery. The longer I sat and talked with him I could tell this guy was real uncomfortable with me being so comfortable working there. The following Monday morning I got a call, they told me thank you so much, and then they said the regular guy had showed up for work. I thought it was funny in spite of the fact my feelings were right on target. It was a nice little stretch while it lasted, and I knew it would be short lived so it wasn't any kind of a shock. I was adapting to this life style, time to get yourself back to looking again.

Along the way, during this period of time, Someone I had been connected with called on me to see if I could find a good deal for him on some used flat bed trailers. I just happened to know where there were just what he was looking for. I went to where the trailers were, and struck up a potential deal for two trailers. I knew the prices were right. I went back to the potential buyer explained everything, he was real high on me making the deal. I made the

The Cool Apple Express

offer, it was taken, I used the buyers tractor, took over a check, closed the deal, and hauled the two trailers to the buyer. Everyone one is happy, including me, not to mention I made a worthy sum for myself. Made up for any shortfall of work during that particular time period.

The part-time jobs were coming along at the right times and was managing to keep myself busy and my head above water. I sold my nice boat and put the money in the bank. I bought that boat brand new and had it 8 years. I didn't need the boat sitting there and not using it, and I had a serious buyer that would pay what I wanted, so I sold it. It was a slight downer in a way, I had always been a big Salmon fisherman, but it was the practical thing to do and when things got more consistent job wise, I could always buy me another if I wanted one.

There were a couple places I tried extra hard to get on with, kind of frustrating at times to not get hired. Meanwhile, I seem to come up with these part-time jobs that would seem to be there when I needed them and things would keep on trucking along. I got a call from Harvey Richardson., he had been the major tool in my hiring at Lone Star, outside of my obvious trucking talents, and he was now with Salmon Bay Sand & Gravel. I was kind of surprised when he called me into drive there, especially with all the BS I was involved in at Lone Star, even though it wasn't between he & I. I was in the sack when he called my house and I told him I would be right over. Driving is driving, but working at Salmon Bay was a lot different than Lone Star even though they performed the same job in the same city. Salmon Bay was a family run, little smaller outfit. They did mostly small, and a lot of home owner jobs. They did a lot of work on Queen Anne Hill! Harvey started calling me pretty regular and I tried to be as much of an asset as I could. I knew when I had accumulated my 400 hours they would quit calling me and that coincided with me having to have the plate surgically removed from my injured leg in Dec. 1988, two years after I had broken it in half. That worked out fine and I would start off 1989 not being able to work until the third week in January.

I had applied to Boeing Trucking as soon as I was able to be released for work from the Doctor in June 1987. I had checked in with some people I knew at Boeing Trucking from time to time but I didn't get any encouragement. I knew from my contacts at the Teamsters Hall that they were putting people on. I was trying to stay persistent without looking like some kind of a fool. Going into year two since I had applied for the job at Boeing and… no action! I have to thank my friend Tim Sullivan, who now, was a business agent at the Teamsters. Boeing was not his account, but he asked the agent that was, "why can't Mike get his foot in the door"? There is no way of knowing for sure, but I personally think that was a big help. So… I'm out there and I'm finding work and jumping on it.

I went into a place called Bloch Steel and told them I was looking for work. It was about the first week in March, and they told me they could use me. Bloch Steel, another one of those not so fancy places, but, they treated me fine, I would get dirty, they paid me good, and so were the checks. The man that owned the place was a really nice elderly person. I had been working there extra, steady, for a short time and he came out smiling and introduced himself to me. That was a breath of fresh air. He made a good first impression with me, and that carries a lot of weight. I did a lot of different things, but I think the main job I did was haul flatbed trailer loads of scrap iron out to a place in Kent, where you parked yourself where guided, and sat to wait your turn to get off loaded. This large crane with a big magnet came over the trailer and started lifting off all the iron till you were empty. Not a real brain drain.

The people I came in contact with at Bloch Steel were all O K. No problems with the help, and then one day in April, I was called over and told they were going to put me on steady. I told them I was grateful, the owner was there and I thanked him, and after all this… the very next day Boeing said they were going to hire me after I had taken a student trip with one of their trucks, and passed. I really felt good, and I was totally relieved, but, I felt bad about having to tell Bloch Steel I wouldn't be staying there. I did tell them, and they acted disappointed, and I tried to tell them my short stay there was fine. It was two years that I had applied to work at Boeing Trucking, and now, it finally was really going to happen. The long Rocky road from Sea Bay would now start to smooth out and that was a welcoming feeling to say the least. When things don't come easy, it builds character, so… I must have a ton of character by now.

WORKING AT BOEING TRUCKING

Northbound at the Everett Scale House 1995

I ARRIVED AT THE gate to Boeing Trucking on 19 June, 1989, my badge, that was suppose to be at the gate, was lost. The gate called in to Supervisor Ken Bowden and he came to the gate to walk me in. I can remember the exact words I told him, "I am real happy to be here". He was in a real positive mood and I would find out that he was one of the real good guys at Boeing Trucking, actually the best person in management I would ever know there. We talked briefly along the way to the office, and after some basic directions, I went about the business of taking it all in and trying to immediately adapt to what I was suppose to do in the form of work. The dispatcher on duty just happened to be someone I had known, and he was one of the first people I had to check in with.

Boeing was probably one of the first words I ever learned to say. I grew up, and was raised right on the top of Boeing Hill from the time I was 2 until I was 16 years old. A lot of people in my neighborhood had worked at Boeing, we had two complete wars during that 14 year period of time, WWII, and the Korean War. I watched the maiden flights of the B-47; B-52, and the 747, up until this day, I had never worked at Boeing and I was 51 years old. I had driven down E. Marginal Way about a zillion times, passing all the Boeing facilities, taking everything for granted as far as what was inside the fences, now, I had to learn where all the stuff was, and in the beginning, that was a time consuming job in itself. I was told by a reliable source, get a Boeing directory, tear out all the maps and put them on your clip board, and that was the best thing to do.

My impression of morale in the trucking section, when I arrived, was really positive. If you pulled in with a load, and lets say, another driver was idle for a moment, and you might not even know that driver, more often than not, that driver would come over to your trailer and immediately start helping you untie your load. It was classy, it was infectious I think, and made for a great attitude to break down barriers. You almost got the impression it was recreation instead of work. I loved it, and you gotta know, if you have been in the trucking business very long, so many people are so insecure in so many places, you come in as a stranger, you are automatically considered a threat at a lot of places. That was not the case when I came to work at Boeing, we all know, people are going to have trouble with people, and of course, Boeing was no exception, but trucking at Boeing was cool, for the most part. I'm sure Ken Bowden's influence had a lot to do with that.

They broke me in the first couple weeks on day shift, and then… I was assigned a 3rd shift job starting at mid-night. I wanted to get off those hours as fast as I could. For the two weeks I was on that shift, I hardly slept. I had a chance to go to 2nd shift General semi out of Plant II, and I jumped on it immediately. I ended up staying on that shift for 6 ½ years. There was several times I could have gone to first shift, but one factor about 2 nd shift, it allowed me to work full time, and then, the full time 2nd job I had, taking care of my Mother, it worked out great. I was able to keep Mom in her house and not bring that responsibility into my work place. I would arrange her doctor appts. for in the morning hours and head for work about 1:30 in the afternoon. All the time I was at Boeing, there were only a very few times that taking care of Mom interrupted things for me at work.

The worst time I had a problem with Mom, while I was working at Boeing, came in late August 1993. I was about a little over an hour from getting off work, and thank God I wasn't going over the mountain that night. Mom had a stroke in her bed and the college girl I had living there, called work and I raced to her house. The ambulance was getting ready to take her to Northwest Hospital and I followed it over there. It was around mid-night at the time and I stayed at the hospital till around 6 in the morning. The next 5 months would put a lot more strain on me since I was the only person in my family, and I made all the decisions and had to do all the work.

I had put a college girl in Mom's house in April 1993. She lived there for free, kept an eye out for Mom, wash the dishes once in awhile, and I even bought her a car for transportation. It started out good, but slowly went down hill, till it rapidly went down hill. I had advertised at U Dub, she came to my house and I explained in depth what the situation was so there would be no miss-interpretations of what to expect. In addition to all of this, I still went over there every day about 7 in the morning to make sure everything was under control. I took care of all the house & yard maintenance like I always had, and it was just a built in habit that never ended.

It was around the time Mom had the stroke that bigger problems arose with Mom's live in college girl. She kept looking for excuses to not do the little things she had agreed to do and it all boiled over on Christmas eve. I had looked forward to the break at Christmas time for months, like being in a marathon, and then,…the college girl pretty much had a sit down strike on the 23rd of December. I threw her out, let her keep the car, and figured she was way more trouble than she was worth. Instead of having any vacation to re-coup, I got Mom as a full time responsibility again, and I had to make some serious changes. I found out from a therapist about a good nursing home pretty close by and I went to talk with them. It was obvious Mom had to have 24 hour care; I had a full time job responsibility; the people at the nursing home seemed like they would do a good job of helping my Mother. They put Mom on the list and told me it would be at least a month before there would be an opening. I had a barber I knew real well, he was in a situation where he was forced to live in a small room behind the barber shop. I asked him if he would be interested in living over at Mom's house for awhile, and he would have a place to fix his meals, do laundry and have a descent bed. He thought he'd died and went to heaven, and he got along real well with Mom. That would all get put together before I went back to work from the Christmas break.

When I went back to work, things were going along O K at Mom's house and now, I was just waiting for the green light from the nursing home to get my Mother inside where she could have 24 hour care. Now… I had the really big job of convincing Mom what we were going to do. That day came on 19 January 1994, and as I was driving with her in the car to the nursing home… I was doing some heavy talking, and it had to be done for her welfare. Once I

The Cool Apple Express

got her in there, she seemed to adapt pretty darn good, and that was good for me too. She was doing pretty good from the stroke, but was still drooling all the time. Once she got in the home, they went to work fixing her teeth. I had been taking care of her for so long, I would stop by the home about 3 times a week, usually around lunch time, and sit with her while she ate. It was a huge relief for me, and it cut down on a lot of stress in my life that had existed for years.

So, I'm in my first year at Boeing Trucking, 1989, and it's a huge change work wise, to have all this immediate stability and know I would be going to work at the same place, everyday, every week, and not have in the back of my mind, "I'm only a casual worker and today might be my last day". I'll be redundant and say it again, I'm sure when things don't come easy, they aren't handed to you, you definitely appreciate them one hell of a lot more, and at this particular moment, I couldn't be happier.

After being on 2nd shift a very short time, I volunteered for a job that wasn't that popular at that time. It was called "doing the area" which had a multitude of several jobs. All of the people I was working around were all new to me, I didn't know one person before I got there, and of course, you have a period of get acquainted time, they are all checking you out in some way, and you form your impressions individually. The area job I took agreed with me fine and I wound up doing it for an entire year. I called it a "Long Hostlers job". One of the important parts of the job was cleaning out the Salvage Yard, getting those M T trailers up to trucking, checking them thru the shop, if necessary, and getting them either parked for loading or parked on the fence for availability. Boeing Trucking was real busy when I got there and there was never a loss for work for the area guy. I had a food run with a whoopee van; go into Boeing food service, load up food crescents to be unloaded at Boeing Field cafeteria; The Space center cafeteria, and the OxBow. One of the benefits of this job, getting your lunch in the kitchen at Boeing Field from Lou.

Running oversized loads up and down E. Marginal Way, also hauling a dumpster(huge haul) full of garbage to Waste management. The 8 hours went by fast, I was happy about a lot of things and the job was fine with me, I couldn't think of one thing to complain about. After one year I figured I would get back out on the high way, and gave up the job to a real good guy I trained for it, Fletcher Barnes. I had actually earned a weeks vacation for the first time in awhile and took a trip to Hawaii before starting General semi out on the High way.

The last time I had taken a conventional vacation, was in the fall of 1986 and I went to Las Vegas and had a good time. Was winning good the first day, and lost the magic the next 4 days. A normal vacation for me, would be to go Salmon fishing for a couple days, and then, work on a car for 3 to 4 days, and be perfectly happy. It's now early fall of 1990, and I am going to take a vacation to Hawaii like a real tourist, it's really funny to me when I look back… I don't even know how to act like a tourist! I had stopped in Hawaii twice, once in May 1957, and again in Feb. 1959, passing thru Hickam Field going and coming from Okinawa. I had just turned 21 in 1959, and when we had a 3 hour stop in Honolulu on the way back, and I went into the cocktail lounge, sat there downing a couple drinks, I thought I was one real big shot. Little did I know back then I had it made and even though I was doing real adult things, I was really a baby. If I could have isolated myself at the age of 21… that would have been cool.

I didn't really handle the job of a tourist that well. I had 5 days to be one and I never told a soul till this moment, I called Hawaiian Airlines and paid them $100, so I could come back a day earlier. I loved the weather, the physical enviroment, but man… the beaches were packed all the time; everything cost double than the mainland, and buying a bunch of souveniers is just a bunch of crap. Most of the people I saw were eating at McDonalds cause the food was so high. I started each day by walking over to the huge park. Take a cold drink and some good Macadamian Nut cookies. All kinds of birds would land on the picnic table and I would share my cookies with em. They had some good chinning bars on the play field, and I would work out for about 20 minutes, and then, speed walk up to

The Cool Apple Express

Diamond Head and back. Probably would bore the average tourist to death! I wished later I would have visited the "Arizona", but I didn't. So... I had that 5 hour plane ride on that L10-11 back to Sea-Tac. All the Johns located in the rear of the aircraft, not far from my seat, and I smell like I'm riding in a cattle car all the way back. Won't do that again for thrills.

So, I'm a crummy tourist! Must be something inherently wrong when a person wouldn't like to be a tourist. Back from my vacation I started out with going back on the road and leaving the confines of East Marginal Way. I had to be out there with all the crazy traffic every afternoon and night. There was a way to duck out on some of that by running over the mountain to Moses Lake. After you got out of the city and reached Eastgate, it was mostly a battle with the weather as the only real hazzard to deal with. I didn't start running Moses Lake right away, but once I volunteered to go, I would make one to two trips a week the entire time I was at Boeing. It would be nice to run with someone you liked, but that didn't happen all the time. Once you were over the summit of Snoqualmie, the company radio was out of reach and you could communicate with the other driver and talk all the way over to Moses Lake.

There were so many trips over time that most of them run together when you think back except for a few outstanding ones. Could have been the winter of 1993. A real cold snowy winter on the eastside of the mountain. Once we got to the turn at mile marker 176 on I-90, you would make a left turn that would go past the truck stop. Always looking at first for the neon sign that would show the outside temp. It seemed like every nite I went by that sign it would be around 8 below zero, the same sign that might say 105 degrees above zero in July. Week after week and it stayed that way all winter over there. On a particular night, I was running along with this older guy I knew, we had come off Vantage, the road was iced over in spots, but the ice fog was pea soup. We got up the hill on the other side of the river and from there, it's about 38 miles left to Moses Lake. I was in the rear, the other driver was in front, we had a white knuckle driver between us, the road was really iced over now, and with the pea soup ice fog, and not knowing what that car in front of me was going to do next... it was a thrill a second. I was on the radio with the other driver, and he and I both had outrageous coughs. We made it to the cut off at mile marker 176, and that was partial relief.

When we finally got out to Larsen AFB, there is no one there at that time of night. We were calling it "Ice Station Zebra' because of the snow buildup, and when you arrived there at night, you never knew if there would be a path in the snow going out to the loading area where the trailers were. Sometimes, you had to blaze your own trail hoping you wouldn't get stopped and have to chain up just to get across the area. On this particular night, soon as both of us got out of our tractors and that cold air hit our lungs, with the coughs we had, we both started really hacking. We got our trailers untied and then got hooked up to the back loads and got them tied down. While we were doing all this, we were talking back and forth about the terrible viruses we had. Well... that was the thought for the moment, but that wasn't what was really taking place. Mine was a virus. Evidently, his was more serious because, right after we got back in town, he was diagnosed with Cancer and died within 3 months. Things like that seem to stay with you forever.

One evening, just as it was getting dark, I went into the yard south of Renton to get a full load of landing gears going to Paine Field in Everett. Traffic was still pretty heavy on I-405 when I reached there, so I was trucking along at a pretty moderate speed. It's a routine run, got a couple million dollars worth of freight on the trailer, watching the important traffic as usual and just making my way to the next stop. I was just south of Bellevue by a couple miles and my instincts were sending me a message to check out the pick-up, with the camper, that was running along side of me with a cab light on. I unconsciously looked down into the window of the pick-up and all of a sudden I wasn't unconscious anymore.

The driver was a guy, stretched across the seat was a woman with her head in his lap. She was on her back with her legs propped up and spread pretty wide. She was naked and was stroking her

The Cool Apple Express

clitoris with the nail from her middle finger. My heart rate must have increased from 60 beats per minute to about 200 beats per minute in a heart beat. I can't believe to this day how aroused I became instantly after seeing this. Soon as they knew I was hooked, the intensity to arouse me increased.

I'm traveling along at about 60mph: I have a valuable load of freight on my trailer; I'm coming in to the edge of Bellevue with I-90 traffic merging with my northbound traffic; I'm trying to be conscious of all the traffic and I can't take my eyes off the pick-up. When I had to slow down, they accommodated me by slowing down too, so I wouldn't miss out on anything. It wasn't till we were past Bellevue, that they finally disappeared. When I pulled into the trucking area at Paine Field, my heart was still pounding like hell. I went up the stairs to the dispatch to tell all the people up there what just had happened. I probably looked like some kind of fool at the time, but, but, but, I guess it was just a normal reaction. I thought about that several times after that happened. Yes folks, it really does happen!

An incident happened one night that I will never forget. I have no answer as to what started the whole thing, it just came out of the blue. It's a constant reminder that, there are evil people out there in this world and you can come in contact with them at any moment. I was coming out of Paine Field with a double drop empty low boy trailer. I had just dropped off an engine and was headed back to the Powerpack & Strut yard that was south of Renton. I was just north of Bellevue on I-405 when this guy whips in front of me and slammed on the brakes. I was watching the road closely and when it originally happened, I figured he was just another crazy driver. I became real conscious of this guy and he had some kind of a plan. No matter what lane I got in he was going to slid in front of me and slam on his brakes. This went on for several miles over and over again. It was another time when it was real hard to control my emotions. It was so tempting to mash the pump and run right over the top of the guy. Your mind does a lot of thinking, wondering why some asshole is doing this. He took a Renton off ramp and threw out the finger as he was going off. I can only assume he hated Boeing, I was the lucky guy that came along at the right time. It's something you never have the answer for.

Lots of stuff is routine, busy, but pretty routine. I had been at Boeing for a year and a half, and was asked to be involved in a special move one night. Boeing was moving a real wide load out of Shelton to the Space Center in Kent. The load was 22 feet wide and would consist of 2 semi loaded flatbeds. My job was to take a pilot car and be part of the main body that was a convoy. I think there was about 10 Pilot cars involved, and one whole lot of Washington State Patrol vehicles.

We first had to head out of this rural place, near Shelton, on a rural 2 lane road that probably went over 10 miles. We then intersected with the high way that leaves Olympia and eventually winds up at the coast. We made a left on that and it took us to I-5 where we merged to go northbound. That gave our convoy some elbow room and that is where the State Patrol had to use all of their vehicles. A certain group of vehicles would leap frog the on/off ramps like this. One group would go ahead of us to the very next on ramp and block it completely. We would pass by with our entire convoy and the group of WSP vehicles following behind would pull out to the left, race by us to the next on ramp and block that one. The WSP vehicles at the last one would fall in behind. We did that all the way to Kent, probably about 50 miles on I-5. We dropped off that pretty steep hill with a pretty tight turn that took us down to the valley and into the Space Center. It came off beautiful and also a lot faster than I would have thought. We had gotten into the Space Center about 1:OOAM, and do not think there were any negative problems along the way. Because I was involved in being part of it, there was no way I would have known what it looked like but, I looked at the news on T V, and they had a clip of our convoy on the freeway and it looked real impressive.

There was really unconscious luck involved when it came to weather. That took place on the 18th of Dec. 1990, and it was unusually warm that night, in the 50's. Exactly 24 hours later, the

Pacific Northwest would be hit hard with a major snow storm and really cold temps that would stick around for weeks. We would have 3 or 4 days to deal with that crummy weather before we went on our yearly Christmas break. The first night of the storm, I made a trip to Everett and then spent the rest of the night helping in the area and on the avenue. It was a real mess! The second night, my first trip to Everett took 4 hours. I can remember being on I-5 northbound near the downtown area and I-5 was freaked out. I didn't want to stop and not be able to get started again and have to chain up in that mess. It came close more than a few times. The next couple of nights were really bad too, but I think so many people were burnt out from the night before, they just stayed home. Finally came the Christmas break and a week of relief, couldn't have come at a better time.

One of the neat things about working at Boeing was the visit by the "Blue Angels" every year for SeaFair. They were staged right across the street from trucking on Boeing Field. I never get tired of seeing their equipment, their planes and the things they can do. Many times I would motor by their stuff on the field while driving a semi and that was always entertainment for me. Way back in 1957 when I was stationed at Onna Point on Okinawa, I was doing a 3rd shift and was sacked out in my bunk. They came in the barracks and rousted us outta the sack in the middle of the day. When I got out in front of the barracks they had a party going on with free beer & hot dogs. I don't remember what we were celebrating but the "Air Force Thunderbirds" flew up the island from Kadena A F B and flew overhead in their brand new F-100 Super Saber's. Real impressive stuff for me. I was only 19 then, and precisioned flying teams like the "Thunderbirds" were still pretty much in their infancy. Things I will remember all my life.

On the 2nd of January 1995, I turned 57 years old and that coincided with a full elgibility for a Teamster pension. Boy... it was really tempting to jump on that but first, I had some thinking and planning to do, and try to be smart. I came from a family with a huge work ethic. I do not know anyone in my family that ever retired. My Dad had served in 2 world wars; worked some high profile jobs like; running the Hollywood theatre for Jack Warner in the 1930's. A couple years after he was discharged from the Marine Corps at the end of WWII, my Dad ran the Inglewood Golf & Country Club out in Juanita. After that, he ran some well known club in San Francisco that had a live broadcast on the radio. He died at the age of 57 in the Veterans Hospital in Walla Walla in March 1955. I took my very first plane ride when I flew to Southern, California for his funeral. Buried in a Veterans cemetery near UCLA. My poor Mother outlived two husbands that died long before she did, and she was divorced from both of them, didn't plan one cent for any kind of retirement. She just figured she would work teaching dancing till she tipped over. I have no idea what she would do if I hadn't been there to support her the last years of her life. It could have been real ugly. My Grandpa, I lived with him from the time I was 2 till I was sixteen. I had just turned sixteen, and I remember the day I dressed him, put him into a Yellow Cab and sent him to the West Seattle General Hospital. He would never see the inside of his house again. He had lung cancer from smoking all his life. A work ethic to end all work ethics. To have lung cancer in 1954 was an immediate death sentence. I was in the 2 nd half of my Sophomore year at West Seattle High, and I would walk down to the junction to visit Grandpa on the way home. He showed his appreciation for me in a different way then, and when I look back in time, I'm real glad I had the common sense to do that. I would catch the city bus from there and ride home to Holden street. Maybe work behind the counter in the store for a few hours before locking up. My Mother was having so much trouble dealing with it, she would stay away for days at a time. I had to think on my feet. With Grandpa out of circulation, what there was of my family was shot down. I had to grow up fast in a lot of ways, but when I think back, I didn't know any better. Nobody told me I was suppose to have someone there supporting me, or I couldn't survive. When school started in the fall, I went to live at the Hi School and Monastery, St Martins in Lacey, Washington. It was the best thing that could have ever happened to me. I thank God to this day for that.

The Cool Apple Express

Some time early in 1994, the two guys running the fuel farm at Boeing Field, Chuck & Rich, asked me if I would be interested in being their back up. I was Plant II General Semi and there was no way I wanted to leave my position. They were looking for someone to come in and be able to work on the farm if one of them was off sick, and, so they could take some free time. They worked every day, and they had 3 guys working that shift but when Don Counts passed away, Boeing did not replace him and it didn't give them much slack. I told them if it didn't affect my job, I would come in as a back up when needed. So... I studied for the test to be a fuel driver, and those two guys along with Paul over at Renton, did a real good job of preparing me for the test I had to take to be a fueler. I aced the test, and for the rest of my time at Boeing, I would occasionally fill in there and also at Renton field.

Just before the roll out of the 777 in 1995, I came into work one afternoon and got into my tractor, and was ready to load up and get out on the High Way. Someone told me to high tail it across the street to the fuel farm, no one was there. I got over there and they were right, I had no idea where Chuck & Rich were. I no sooner got there and these Boeing people showed up, they told me they wanted me to set up some tankers for a fuel test. I kept looking around for the regular guys cause I didn't know what these people really wanted. When they didn't show up, I had to try to look responsible, so... I winged it! I told them to describe to me exactly what they wanted and where I was suppose to set this equipment up. After they described the arrangement, I went around the yard, found some empty old tankers, and hoses, and proceeded to set up what would be a fuel test site, and it was done. It must have come out fine, it remained exactly the way I set it up, for days. In June 1995, we were all given a Special Team Achievement award for that particular fuel test for the new 777. I felt good about it, why shouldn't I? The 777 became a very successful aircraft for Boeing.

It was at this time that Boeing was offering some real good deals for their people to retire. We, in the trucking part of Boeing (Teamsters), we were not covered by that plan, that came under the Machinists Union. For me personally, I had no complaints at all. Everything I had at Boeing in the form of pay and benefits was just fine. My Teamsters pension was now available to me and it was up to me to decide when I wanted to pull out. I had a lady friend that worked first shift at an office in Renton. I only got to see her once a week, working different shifts. She took her retirement in the summer of 1995. I made the decision to take mine 1 October 1995. I had part-time work waiting for me the day that I took my Teamster retirement. A lot of people talk about how someone in their family was the first to go to college. I was the first in mine to take an official retirement.

It was a secure feeling to have, and also know, I would continue to work at another pace and also be able to do things for me personally.

Life would not end there, but my trucking career would. I did drive part time, but also did a lot of other things. When I see a beautiful new Peterbilt cruising down the High way on a nice day, I think, it would be nice to do that once in awhile for one day, and then put it away. To all the other people out there pushing the High way, "KEEP ON TRUCKIN".

EPILOGUE

On a very personal note, I can be very critical, I can be very complimentary. I came to work at BOEING Trucking at the age of 51. I know I had faced age discrimination by that time of my life but, I wasn't an activist person in that regard. I might think a lot about it but, I would suck it up and move on. I seen early on, while I was at Boeing that, they did not do age discrimination. Before, around the time I was hired, and after, Boeing brought in several people in my age group and it was real noticeable to me. Where other companies noticeably used age discrimination and it was real obvious, Boeing Trucking seemed more interested in hiring people with actual experience. Of course there was a certain amount of nepotism that went on, and the experienced hands use to laugh about how Joe was able to get his nephew little Johnny a job. Boeing was not Utopia, but it was an excellent place to be, doing what I was doing during that time period. I appreciated the opportunity to work there the 6 ½ years that I did before taking my full retirement from the Teamsters. A real big thanks for the benefits I received. It allowed me to support my Mother, who had very little income, and to actually retire when I did.

I've always admired people that had the ideal family, guys that went to work and worked for one employer till retirement. I never came within one million miles of either. Sometimes you have to overcome so many things over the course of your life that your closet is plenty full by the time you're up there. If you are satisfied with yourself for basically being a fair and good person, and I know I am, only you really know the score about yourself. It doesn't matter what some person congers up about you, and some do, you have to just let that stuff roll off your knife and move forward with self assurance.

Another thing that I thought about a lot over the years while in the trucking business. Take 2 different jobs. Both jobs are good jobs to work. I'm talking about LASME and Lone Star. They were both good Teamster jobs and for the most part, you had blue collar people that could have been interchangeable working those jobs. Why???... one job, working at LASME, had good management people that worked well with the drivers. I never saw petty bickering, none of the drivers and dock people were trying to hold up the company. A pleasant place to work for me, all the time.

The actual work at Lone Star was fine. The management was always in a state of mind, especially after the strike of 1980, like it was a me versus them attitude, management against the drivers. I tried to be friendly with Stan B., he made it impossible. He didn't want any form of congeniality to exist whatsoever. As for them bringing in a person like Michael P. to be in management. It wouldn't take a genius to figure out who this guy was. All the drivers knew. Why would a company want to run on that kind of basis?

It's all behind me now. It's pretty much meaningless at this point. The good; the bad; the ugly! Working for LASME and Boeing, it was good. Some of the casual places I worked for were good too. They were a Port in the storm and helped along the way. Got to mention the Teamsters Hiring Hall too. It was something that, over the years that I used it, was a good thing for me. Driving for Joe at Little Audrey off & on all those years,...some of those trips in the dead of winter were really tuff but, it was good to have that Ace—in-the-Hole and always know, no matter how bad things could get job wise, "you always had a job working for Joe if you needed it." Driving for C F Tanklines should have been good. The crew and most of the management were good to work with but, driving that terrible equipment and hauling hazardous materials with it,...it was bad for me. The management at Lone Star was ugly. It didn't need to be that way but, it was. That's only my opinion. I don't speak for anyone else. I just call it the way I saw it. A lot of those trips I made to Chicago for Joe in the wintertime. Leave mile marker 43 east bound at Denny Creek and not see any asphalt till you get back because of the ice & snow. There wasn't any other thing in my life that made me more tired than that. Nothing!!

I would like to insert my favorite picture of my Mother. It was taken in 1940 looking south on 13th S W and Holden street next to Turner's Grocery where I was raised from the time I was 2, till I was 16 years old. Notice 13th S W was just a dirt and gravel road in those days.

Lillian Turner—Mother

www.ingramcontent.com/pod-product-compliance
Lightning Source LLC
Chambersburg PA
CBHW030326080526
44584CB00012B/724